THE

PUBLICATIONS

OF THE

Lincoln Record Society

FOUNDED IN THE YEAR

1910

VOLUME 91

ISSN 0267–2634

THE LETTER BOOK OF
SIR ANTHONY OLDFIELD

1662–1667

EDITED BY

P. R. SEDDON

The Lincoln Record Society

The Boydell Press

First published 2004

A Lincoln Record Society Publication
published by The Boydell Press
an imprint of Boydell & Brewer Ltd
PO Box 9, Woodbridge, Suffolk IP12 3DF, UK
and of Boydell & Brewer Inc.
668 Mt Hope Avenue, Rochester, NY 14620, USA
website: www.boydellandbrewer.com

ISBN 0 901503 68 1

A catalogue record for this book is available
from the British Library

Details of other Lincoln Record Society volumes are available
from Boydell & Brewer Ltd

This publication is printed on acid-free paper

Typeset by Pru Harrison, Woodbridge, Suffolk
Printed in Great Britain by
Antony Rowe Ltd, Chippenham, Wiltshire

CONTENTS

ACKNOWLEDGEMENTS

I am grateful to the Syndics of Cambridge University Library for permission to publish document Dd.ix.43, and to Professor David Smith for commissioning me to edit it for the Lincoln Record Society. My special thanks are due to Dr Alison McHardy for persuading me to undertake the work. I am very grateful to Dr Nicholas Bennett, the General Editor, for his careful assistance in preparing the document for publication.

ABBREVIATIONS

BL	British Library
CCC	M. A. Everett Green (ed.), *Calendar of the Proceedings of the Committee for Compounding etc.* (5 vols, London, 1889–1892).
CSPD	M. A. Everett Green (ed.), *Calendar of State Papers, Domestic Series, of the Reign of Charles II, 1660–1685* (28 vols, London, 1860–1947).
CTB	W. A. Shaw (ed.), *Calendar of Treasury Books 1660–[1718]* (32 vols, London, 1904–1969).
CUL	Cambridge University Library
DNB	L. Stephen (ed.), *The Dictionary of National Biography* (63 vols, London, 1885–1900).
HMC	Historical Manuscripts Commission
LA	Lincolnshire Archives
Maddison	A. R. Maddison (ed.), *Lincolnshire Pedigrees* (4 vols, Harleian Society l, li, lii and lv, 1902–06).
OB	P. R. Seddon (ed.), *The Letter Book of Sir Anthony Oldfield.*
Oxford, Bodl.	Bodleian Library, Oxford
PC	Privy Council
PRO	Public Record Office
SP	State Papers

INTRODUCTION

THE MANUSCRIPT

Manuscript C.Dd.ix.43 in Cambridge University Library appears to have been intended by its original owner, Sir Anthony Oldfield, to be a commonplace book. The inscription on the waste leaf notes that it was begun 8 October 1660 at Grantham. The first entries are drawings of the coats of arms of Charles Bolles of Louth and Sir William Carr of Sleaford. These arms could have been produced for the 1634 visitation of Lincolnshire for on pages v and vi there is a list of men distrained at these proceedings and a note that the claim of John Burton was respited for better proof of arms.[1] There are two undated letters before the entry of instructions from the Earl of Southampton, Lord Treasurer, to Oldfield to raise an assessment. The letter is dated 1 January 1662 (all dates in this edition have been given in new style). It is followed by a letter to Mr Harvie of 21 February 1662.[2] The arrangement of the letters is the first indication that correspondence was not always entered in chronological order. Letters to, among others, Sir Marmaduke Gresham, Oldfield's brother-in-law, are followed by an undated letter to the Bishop of Lincoln.[3] A letter of 'Dear Nick' about the ordinary material of letters intervenes[4] before the commencement of letters about articles presented against Robert Peirson, rector of Spalding, which can be found in Appendix Two. There is also a record of a dispute about tithes during the incumbency of Robert Ram, Peirson's predecessor.[5] It is not until page 18 that the first letter on militia business can be found. The first dated letters about the militia are from January 1663. A letter to the Earl of Lindsey, lieutenant of the Lincolnshire militia, on pages 25–26 is out of chronological order for it was written on 21 January 1664.[6] It is followed by a heading to Mr Phabian Philips but the content of the letter was never entered. After a letter to Mr Ralph[7] there are eleven blank pages. From the letter of Oldfield to Mr Edward Christian of 17 July 1663 militia business dominates the entries. Occasionally letters about the raising of taxation intervene[8] and there are three lists of the King's ships with the numbers of men

---

[1] Maddison, ix, 228–9, for a genealogy of the Carrs which shows that Sir William died in 1606. The records of the 1634 visitation were incorporated in Maddison's pedigrees.

[2] CUL C.Dd.ix.43, pp. 1–2. The pagination is by Roman numerals until this letter from Southampton when Arabic numerals begin and continue until the end of the manuscript.

[3] Apart from the letter to the Bishop of Lincoln (OB 82), this correspondence is not included in the edition.

[4] CUL C.Dd.ix.43, p. 8.

[5] OB 83–86, the records of the tithe disputes (CUL C.Dd.ix.43, pp. 22–23), have not been transcribed.

[6] OB 1–4, 22.

[7] CUL C.Dd.ix.43, p. 29.

[8] These letters, with the exception of one to Sir Edward Barkham, can be found in Appendix One (OB 74–81).

and guns.[9] After page 142 the pages are left blank until page 212 when a diverse series of entries begins. A list of the benefactors of Spalding Library is followed by a catalogue of the books in the Library and a list of the volumes in Oldfield's study.[10] Pages 233–5 record the manner of planting vineyards at Bacharach. A decision of the justices about the liability for road repairs is noted and proposals from the farmers of the Hearth Tax to the justices for the Holland division are recorded.[11] The only militia business at the end of the book (in Appendix Four)[12] is a list of Oldfield's troop and lists probably of men who were in the volunteer troops of Sir Edward Barkham and Sir Philip Harcourt, and a receipt for money paid for fourteen day duty in 1667. Two letters written towards the end of the siege of Newark are entered, as are lists of towns within four miles of Stamford and Horncastle.[13] A 'littanie' to be read at every election and a certificate made 'one night in mirth' complete the entries.[14] The vast majority of the entries are records of militia business and explain why the book is often known as the Oldfield militia book.

THE OLDFIELDS OF SPALDING

It was through Anthony Oldfield, who died in 1635, that the family became associated with Spalding. In 1609 Anthony Oldfield, who came from Bingley, York-shire,[15] purchased from the crown the advowson of the rectory of St Mary and St Nicholas church, Spalding. In March 1620 these rights were transferred to feoffees who included John, the son of Anthony.[16] John Oldfield was a dedicated supporter of Charles I in an area where, apart from Crowland, there was little support for the King.[17] John joined the Newark garrison and was present at its surrender in May 1646. It was not until October 1647, after the payment of a composition fine of £1,390, that he was restored to his estates.[18] Oldfield appears to have lived quietly under the subsequent regimes for he did not come to the attention of the authorities. However in 1659 Gervase Holles included him in the list of the lords and gentry of Lincolnshire who might be serviceable to the King. The plans for a rising in Lincolnshire in the summer of 1659 came to nothing.[19] In November 1659, after his father's death, Anthony Oldfield succeeded to the estates. The son of John by Mary, daughter of John Blythe of Denton, he was baptized in Spalding church on 27 July 1626. The disruption of the first civil war probably explains the deferment of his enrolment at Grays Inn until 6 May

---

9   CUL C.Dd.ix.43, pp. 73–5, 86–92, 255–60 (the lists have not been transcribed).
10   CUL C.Dd.ix.43, pp. 213, 215–17, 223–5 (the catalogue has not been transcribed).
11   OB 80, 81.
12   CUL C.Dd.ix.43, pp. 239–40 (the lists have been transcribed in Appendix Four).
13   CUL C.Dd.ix.43, pp. 252–3, 265–66 (this correspondence and lists have not been transcribed).
14   CUL C.Dd.ix.43, pp. 240–1, 268.
15   A genealogy of the family can be found in Maddison, 735–8.
16   M. Brassington (ed.), St. Mary and St. Nicholas, Spalding (Spalding, 1984), 16–17; LA Measure MS 3/1/21.
17   C. Holmes, *Seventeenth Century Lincolnshire* (Lincoln, 1980), 163.
18   *CCC* 1296; BL Add. MS 25,302, fo 141r.
19   BL Egerton MS 2541, fo 362; D. Underdown, *Royalist Conspiracy in England, 1649–1660* (New Haven, 1960), 242, 271.

1647.[20] How long he spent in his legal training is unclear but he became an attorney and steward of the Duchess of Somerset.[21] The date of his first marriage and the christian name of his wife and father-in-law have eluded genealogists but she was the daughter of Parke of Fleet, Lincolnshire, and before her death bore him four children who did not survive. In 1658 he married Elizabeth Gresham, daughter of Sir Edward Gresham of Limpsfield, Surrey; his son and heir John was born of her in October 1659. In August 1660 he was among the many whose fathers' service to the late King was rewarded by a knighthood and baronetcy. Oldfield's name is absent from the Lincolnshire men nominated in the late summer of 1660 for selection by the King as deputy lieutenants.[22] He was appointed to the commission of the peace for the Holland district of the shire and in the autumn of 1661 he became sheriff of Lincolnshire.[23] In July 1662 he was appointed a deputy lieutenant.[24] It is the correspondence generated by his work as a deputy lieutenant which forms the bulk of this edition.

THE LINCOLNSHIRE MILITIA

The restored monarchy needed a military force for its defence and the maintenance of internal security. Before the civil wars internal defence had been the duty of the militias established in the shires and the leading towns.[25] The control of the militia had become, in 1642, a central and unresolved dispute between King and Parliament.[26] At the restoration the statutory basis of the militia was uncertain. The repeal of the 1558 militia statute in 1604 with the subsequent failure to pass amending measures left antiquated legislation dating back to the statute of Winchester of 1258 as the residual authority.[27] In the summer of 1660 the crown, by its prerogative, assumed direction of the militia and began to appoint lieutenants and deputies. As the actions of the lieutenancy were challenged in law a statutory settlement of the militia was an urgent necessity.[28] In the first session of the Cavalier Parliament, when disputes about the rating of

[20] J. Foster (ed.), *The Register of Admissions to Grays Inn* (London, 1889), p. 244; CUL C.Dd.ix.43, pp. 223–5 shows that books on legal matters formed a substantial part of Oldfield's library.
[21] G. E. Cokayne, *Complete Baronetage* (6 vols, Exeter, 1900–09), iii. 104.
[22] Maddison, 737; *Complete Baronetage* iii. 194; PRO SP 29/11/168. It is probable that he was the Anthony Oldfield the younger appointed to the Lincolnshire militia commission in March 1660; C. H. Firth and R. S. Rait (eds), *Acts and Ordinances of the Interregnum* (3 vols, London, 1911), ii. 1435.
[23] BL Egerton MS 2557, fos 48v–49r; Add. MS 36,781, fo 53rv. Oldfield is not included in A. Hughes (comp.), *List of Sheriffs for England and Wales, from the earliest times to 1831* (New York, 1963), 81.
[24] LA Yarborough MS 8/2/5.
[25] L. O. J. Boynton, *The Elizabethan Militia 1558–1638* (London, 1967); A. Fletcher, *Reform in the Provinces: the government of Stuart England* (London, 1986), 282–316.
[26] L. G. Schwoerer, ' "The Fittest Subject for a King's Quarrel": an essay on the militia controversy, 1641–2', *Journal of British Studies* xi (1971), 45–76.
[27] A. Hassell Smith, 'Militia Rates and Militia Statutes 1558–1663' in P. Clark, A. G. R. Smith and N. Tyacke (eds), *The English Commonwealth 1547–1640: Essays in politics and society presented to J. Hurstfield* (Leicester, 1979), 93–110.
[28] Fletcher, *Reform in the Provinces*, 318–19; J. R. Western, *The English Militia in the Eighteenth Century: the story of a political issue, 1660–1802* (London, 1965), 10–11.

contributions prevented a settlement, a temporary militia bill had to be passed.[29] In the next session of Parliament the settlement was delayed by the strong opposition of the Commons to the crown's proposals to raise a standing force for defence.[30] It was not until 17 May 1662 that the act[31] for the ordering of the forces in several counties of the kingdom was passed. In 1663 an additional act[32] amended and made additions to this statute. These two statutes provided the legal framework and directions for the work of the militia. The declaration in 1662 that the 'sole and supreame Power, Government Command and Disposition of the militia' rested with the King settled the dispute of 1642. The monarch had the right to issue commissions of lieutenancy, to appoint and dismiss lieutenants, to give approbation or reject their nominations for deputies. The crown had the power to decide if a tax for the militia, which was restricted to the years 1662–65, should be raised. The determination of the Commons to reject the crown's proposals for permanent forces meant that internal defence rested on the militias raised out 'of the freeholders and persons of interest in the nation'.[33] These were assessed for their contributions to the militia by the lieutenants and deputies, who could also raise a tax for certain items of militia expenditure. The lieutenants inspected the men and their equipment, formed them into military units, and were responsible for their training and their leadership in any action. Ultimately the effectiveness of the militia depended on the work of the lieutenant, his deputies and officers in the shires.

THE LIEUTENANTS AND THEIR DEPUTIES

In July 1660, when the King appointed Montague Bertie, Earl of Lindsey, as lieutenant, the construction of the lieutenancy began. Eventually twenty men were nominated for the crown's approval as deputies.[34] The majority were formerly active royalists or representatives of royalist families. Six nominations reflected the political mood of the times in Lincolnshire. Colonel Edward Rossiter's recent career demonstrates how attitudes had changed among leading Parliamentarians. In the civil wars Rossiter had led Lincolnshire Parliamentarian forces; during the Interregnum he had served in office. By the summer of 1659 he was so disillusioned that he was prepared to join with the royalists to lead a rising in favour of the King. In the next year Rossiter presented to Monck a declaration from the shire in favour of a freely elected Parliament.[35] At the election for the Convention Parliament he was returned with his former Parliamentarian associates Sir Anthony Irby, Sir William Wray and Thomas Hatcher for Lincolnshire constitu-

---

[29] P. Seaward, *The Cavalier Parliament and the Reconstruction of the Old Regime, 1661–1667* (Cambridge, 1989), 141–3; 13 Charles II c.6.
[30] Seaward, *Cavalier Parliament*, 143–51; L. G. Schwoerer, *'No standing armies': the anti-army ideology in seventeenth century England* (London, 1974), 72–94.
[31] 14 Charles II c.3.
[32] 15 Charles II c.4.
[33] C. Robbins, 'Five Speeches, 1661–3, by Sir John Holland MP', *Bulletin of the Institute of Historical Research* xxviii (1955), 198.
[34] PRO SP 29/11/168.
[35] B. D. Henning (ed.), *The History of Parliament, The House of Commons 1660–1690* (3 vols, London, 1983), iii. 351; Holmes, *Lincolnshire*, 216–19; Underdown, *Royalist Conspiracy*, 242, 271.

encies. Sir Edward Ayscough, a leading Lincolnshire Parliamentarian, was also nominated with Sir Michael Armyne, son of Sir William Armyne, member for Grantham, who until 1651 was an active member of the Rump Parliament.[36]

From the nominations the crown chose eleven men to serve as deputies. Four men with a Parliamentarian background and five royalists were omitted.[37] The appointment of Lord Belasyse as lieutenant of the East Riding[38] and the continuation of Lord Willoughby of Parham's interest in the colonial ventures in the West Indies could explain their absence.[39] Some omissions are more difficult to interpret for Lord Widdrington and Rossiter were appointed deputies in 1662. The addition of four men[40] from a royalist background indicates a deliberate decision to establish an overwhelming royalist predominance in the lieutenancy. In August 1660 Secretary Nicholas had made the crown's intentions clear. The militia, he wrote, was to be settled in 'the hands of men of known loyalty'.[41] Increasingly loyalty was being defined as men who had fought for the King or whose families had been royalist. Only Irby and Wray of the deputies came from a Parliamentarian background. The majority of the fifteen appointed deputies were to form the core of the lieutenancy for the next decade.

The career of Montague Bertie, second Earl of Lindsey, demonstrates how royalist credentials could be established. His father, Robert, the first Earl Lindsey, was lieutenant of the shire and a major participant in a syndicate to drain the Fens. Montague served his military apprenticeship in the army of the United Provinces. The first Earl raised a regiment for the King, which fought at Edgehill.[42] In the battle Robert Bertie was killed and his son captured. After his release Lindsey served in the royalist army until the end of the first civil war. He compounded on the Oxford articles, that is, paid a fine for his support of the King. After his composition Lindsey lived quietly though he was once arrested for allegedly plotting against Cromwell.[43] His son, Robert Lord Willoughby d'Eresby, was too young to fight in the war and in 1644 was sent to travel on the continent.[44] Willoughby's deputyship proved to be a preparation for his succession to the office of lieutenant after his father's death in July 1666.

In July 1662 a commission with the authority of the recent statute was issued for Lincolnshire. Montague Bertie, second Earl of Lindsey, was confirmed as lieutenant with twenty-two deputies. Three men were omitted from the previous appointments and ten, who included Widdrington and Rossiter, added to the

36 *House of Commons 1660–90* i. 298–308; B. Worden, *The Rump Parliament, 1648–53* (Cambridge, 1974), 65, 116, 136, 179, 184.
37 PRO SP 29/11/169; Appendix Three.
38 *CSPD 1660–1*, 214; *DNB* ii. 142.
39 Underdown, *Royalist Conspiracy*, 116–17, 136–7, 155, 236–7, 271–2. Parham had been an active supporter of Parliament during the first civil war. As OB 17 shows, by 1663 he had sold his Lincolnshire estates.
40 Appendix Three; Sir Francis Fane, Sir William Thorold, Sir Philip Tirwhitt and Sir Charles Bolles were added to the deputies.
41 PRO SP 29/10/81.
42 K. Lindley, *Fenland Riots and the English Revolution* (London, 1982), 50–55, 144–5; P. Young, *Edgehill 1642: the Campaign and the Battle* (Kineton, 1967), 49, 61.
43 Young, *Edgehill*, 49, 116, 199, 264, 266; *HMC Ancaster* i. 410; *CCC* 1501–4; Underdown, *Royalist Conspiracy*, 163.
44 LA 10 Anc., Lot 349.

former deputies.[45] A comparison with the twelve deputies drawn from the shire's leading families serving with the first Earl of Lindsey shows that the number of deputies had substantially increased.[46] For a shire as large as Lincolnshire it was still a small number but now it was not a man's social status but his support for the King that was the main consideration for appointment. Apart from Lord Willoughby only George Saunderson, Viscount Castleton in the Irish peerage, and Baron William Widdrington of Blankney, were members of the peerage. Widdrington's father, the first baron, a zealous supporter of the King, had his estates confiscated by Parliament when he was proscribed as a traitor, and was killed at Wigan in 1651. His son joined his father in exile and did not return until the restoration of the King.[47] Castleton was too young, as were his nearest family, to fight in the war. In 1659, after being discovered conspiring against the regime, he was imprisoned in the Tower.[48] The lieutenant and seven of his deputies had compounded for the support of the King.[49] Two deputies had compounded along with their fathers.[50] Five deputies were the sons of royalist compounders.[51] Sir Francis Fane does not appear to have been active during the war but his elder brother, the Earl of Westmorland, was a leading royalist and in 1660 was appointed lieutenant of Northamptonshire.[52] For two deputies support for the King in the civil war cannot be established. Sir Martin Lister was the son of Dr Matthew Lister, physician to Henrietta Maria.[53] Sir Thomas Meres was from a leading church family. Robert, his father, was Chancellor of Lincoln cathedral, his mother a niece of John Williams, Bishop of Lincoln and later Archbishop of York.[54] Only Rossiter and Sir William Trollop came from a Parliamentarian background. The appointment of Trollop, sheriff in 1659–60,[55] suggests some consideration was given to increasing the number of deputies in the Holland division. The omission of Sir Anthony Irby left Sir Henry Heron as the only resident deputy. The appointment of Trollop, with Oldfield and Heron, gave a minimum of cover.

Before the commission issued in August 1666,[56] when Robert Bertie was appointed lieutenant, five more men were made deputies. Sir William Wray had

45 LA Yarborough MS 8/2/5; Appendix Three.

46 In Elizabeth's reign there had been four deputies, in James' reign five; in 1629 twelve men were appointed; *HMC Foljambe*, 25; LA Yarborough MS 8/2/2, 3.

47 *DNB* xxi. 184–5; Underdown, *Royalist Conspiracy*, 50.

48 *House of Commons 1660–90* iii. 392–5; Underdown, *Royalist Conspiracy*, 242, 271, 287.

49 The Earl of Lindsey (*CCC* 1501–4); Sir John Monson (*CCC* 1431–2); Sir Philip Tyrwhitt (*CCC* 934, 3488); Sir William Thorold (*CCC* 1331, 4160); Sir John Newton (*CCC* 1388); Sir John Walpole (*CCC* 1379); Sir Edward Dymock (*CCC* 1379); Sir Robert Markham (*CCC* 1044).

50 Henry Heron with his father Sir Edward (*CCC* 1972); Adrian with his father Sir Gervase Scrope (*CCC* 1872); *CSPD 1660–1*, 47.

51 Lord Willoughby, son of the Earl of Lindsey; Sir William Hickman, son of Sir Willoughby (*CCC* 987, 1100); Charles, son of Edward Pelham (*CCC* 1049); Anthony, son of John Oldfield (*CCC* 1296); Lewis, son of Sir Geoffrey Palmer (*CCC* 1433). Sir Thomas Hussey's father, Thomas (member for Grantham) died in 1641; his grandfather, Sir Edward was a compounder (*CCC* 1022–3; *Complete Baronetage* i. 60).

52 Maddison, 343; *DNB* vi. 1042–3.

53 Maddison, 596; *DNB* xi. 1230.

54 *House of Commons 1660–90* iii. 49.

55 *Lists of Sheriffs*, 81; *Complete Baronetage* ii. 158.

56 LA Yarborough MS 8/2/6, appendix three.

been added to the commission by August 1663.[57] In 1664, at Lindsey's request,
Sir John Monson joined his father on the commission, Charles Dymock took his
deceased father's place[58] and by the end of the year Henry Fynes was
appointed.[59] In the next year Sir Robert Carr was made a deputy.[60] By 1667 Sir
Henry Belasyse,[61] who had succeeded Castleton as colonel of the Lindsey regiment, and Sir Philip Tyrwhitt, the fourth baronet, had been made deputies, the
latter taking his late father's place.[62] The addition of Sir Edward Ayscough
completes the appointments in the period under examination.[63] Ayscough and
Wray were the exceptions here, for unlike the majority of the deputies they came
from a Parliamentarian background. In these years the royalist predominance was
maintained.

The Earl of Southampton asked his deputies not to serve as militia officers, for
the crown intended to involve as many 'persons of quality, whose interests were
all fit to be engaged'[64] in these duties. In 1662 the three foot regiments were
commanded by deputies, as was the town company of Lincoln. The Kesteven,
Holland and Lincoln forces continued to be led by deputies.[65] Only two horse
troops, Willoughby's and Oldfield's, were commanded by deputies. Sir John
Monson junior and Sir Philip Tyrwhitt, the fourth baronet, served as horse troop
commanders before they became deputies and continued to hold these positions
after their appointment.[66] Sir Henry Belasyse remained Colonel of the Lindsey
regiment and he also retained command of a horse troop when he was made a
deputy.[67] The number of deputies serving as officers remained a minority of the
lieutenancy. This service had the potential to increase a deputy's knowledge of
the workings and problems of the militia.

After the claim of Montague Bertie, Earl of Lindsey, to be Lord Great
Chamberlain was accepted he spent a substantial part of each year with the
King's court. The Earl would as a result appear to have been an 'absentee'
lieutenant, merely relaying to his deputies the orders of the Privy Council of
which he was a member. Lindsey took steps to prevent his absences affecting the
work of the militia. When the lieutenant and two deputies were ordered to keep
the keys of a chest for the shire's monthly assessment, which was to be stored at
Lincoln, he passed his key to another resident deputy.[68] There are three occasions
which show that from a distance Lindsey kept an informed interest in the work of
the militia and could, when necessary, intervene effectively. In January 1664,

[57] OB 9.
[58] *CSPD 1663–4*, 446. Sir John junior was appointed because of the illness of his father. *House of Commons 1660–90* iii. 79 has Monson senior disabled by ill health and living in Hertfordshire; OB 44, 67 show he was present at meetings in London and Lincoln. Monson senior died in 1683, his son in 1674.
[59] *CSPD 1663–4*, 595.
[60] OB 44.
[61] OB 37, 67; *House of Commons 1660–90* i. 617.
[62] OB 67; *Complete Baronetage* i. 58.
[63] OB 67; Maddison, 58–67; *House of Commons 1660–90* i. 575–6 has a biography of his son and some information about Sir Edward.
[64] Western, *Militia*, 64.
[65] OB 16, 26, 37, 67.
[66] OB 26, 67.
[67] OB 37, 63, 67.
[68] OB 37.

after his examination of the lists of horse troops for Kesteven and Holland, he ordered the deputies to compare the lists with the returns of the parish constables. Lindsey believed on examination they would be able to increase the number of horse without applying the 'extremity' of the statute against those who either defaulted or made insufficient contributions. He ordered eight horses to be transferred from Willoughby's troop to Oldfield's troop and warned his deputies that the numbers in the Kesteven troops had to be increased. After a further review of the lists in July he saw that the numbers in Thorold's troop of horse were less than the 'old' list and he asked for an explanation.[69] A complaint from Sir John Monson that the deputies meeting at Louth had ordered horse from his troop to transfer to Captain Bolles' troop resulted in a decisive intervention by the Lieutenant. In April 1664 Lindsey annulled the order and took the deputies meeting at Louth and Horncastle to task. He reminded the deputies of a previous letter in which they were instructed to prevent the numbers of forces being reduced, by being diligent in their inspection of the value of estates. Any future defaults, he warned, and they would be 'informed of'. Lindsey allowed his deputies a substantial independence in their work but major decisions such as the changes in the lists of troops were to be made only on 'good consideration by the consent of the major part' at a general meeting.[70] The most divisive issue was whether or not the volunteers should be charged for ignoring their obligations to the militia. Resolution of the issue was left until Lindsey visited the shire.[71] Though he was frequently absent from his shire the lieutenant maintained an oversight of the important aspects of the work of the lieutenancy.

Just over a year is an insufficient time to compare and contrast the lieutenancies of Robert, third Earl of Lindsey, with his father's tenure of office. However there are three instances which show that the oversight of the administrative work of the militia was not his major concern. Though he claimed never to have received the request, Lindsey's failure to send lists of his troops to the Council was not an important matter. A far more serious omission was his failure to enforce a rigorous investigation of why Sir Edward Barkham had not sent the bulk of the third monthly pay to the crown. This laxity led to the failure to account for a substantial sum of money. The failure to appoint a treasurer for the weekly pay allowed deficiencies to develop. Lindsey was far more decisive and effective in 1667 when he led his deputies in their defence of the shire.[72]

In Lincolnshire, where decentralisation of quarter sessions and administration was long established, the militia used the customary procedures in its organisation and routine administration. Separate commissions of the peace were issued for Lindsey, Kesteven and Holland.[73] As the letters addressed to the deputies acting in Kesteven and Holland demonstrate, it was accepted that the deputies would concentrate their work within their areas of residence. These were not discrete divisions. As the three resident deputies in Holland included two who commanded its troop of horse and regiment of foot, they had to call on deputies from Kesteven for inspections. The orders of the council and lieutenant were

---

[69] OB 20, 31.
[70] OB 41, 42.
[71] OB 26, 33.
[72] PRO SP 29/134/13; *CSPD 1666–7*, 320; OB 62, 63.
[73] BL Egerton MS 2557, fos 46r–51r; Add. MS 36,781, fos 51r–53v.

transmitted from deputy to deputy within the divisions.[74] The deputies often linked their meetings to quarter sessions, for, as they were all justices, these meetings would give an opportunity for discussion and action. In the two largest districts justices often confined their attendance to the sessions nearest their residences. As a result the deputies in the south of Lindsey based their militia work on the wapentakes which were under the jurisdiction of the Louth and Horncastle sessions.[75] The organisation of the three regiments of foot maintained decentralisation, for they were initially raised from companies based on the wapentakes. Musters and training continued these attitudes: the regiments of foot and companies of horse were mustered within their districts and training was often held in the wapentakes from which the forces originated. As we have seen with a decision taken by the south Lindsey deputies, there was always the danger that decentralisation could give the opportunity for deputies to make decisions which favoured their own area. It was appreciated by the deputies that there were advantages in agreements on one rule and method reached at general meetings. The records of such occasions in the letters suggest that formal regular general meetings were established soon after Lindsey's commission was issued. The practice was to call general meetings only when there was urgent business and, as Oldfield discovered to his cost, the processes of notification could be unsatisfactory.[76] The twice yearly assizes at Lincoln were seen by the deputies as occasions to hold general meetings, for as justices they had an obligation to attend. In April 1665 Lindsey suggested it would be convenient to hold general meetings more frequently since there were certain matters, such as changes in the lists of troops, which should only be made by 'good Consideration by the consent of the Major part of you' at such meetings.[77] In 1666 and 1667 the emergencies and in 1666 the request for information about recusants meant that general meetings had to be held as soon as possible and occasionally, for the convenience of the lieutenant, at Sleaford.[78] Though it was rare for a district not to be represented at a general meeting, the highest number of deputies attending was twelve – just over a half of the commission. The lists of attendees should not be taken as an indication of the activity of the deputies. An analysis of the lists of deputies committing men to jail in 1665 shows that men who were never recorded as attending or who rarely appeared at general meetings were at work in their divisions.[79] The greatest danger of decentralisation was that in times of danger the militia's response would be weakened. At these times the task of the militia was the defence of the shire's coasts. For two of the divisions with their coastline to defend this did not pose a problem. The Kesteven forces also played their part and their activity demonstrates that though organisation and training enhanced the regional characteristics of the militia this did not prevent a countywide response.

[74] OB 48, 54, 55.
[75] OB 41.
[76] OB 19.
[77] OB 26, 30, 37, 41; one meeting in May 1664 was held in London.
[78] OB 49, 54, 57, 62, 63.
[79] PRO SP 29/134/13.

THE ESTABLISHMENT AND ASSESSMENT OF THE MILITIA

The first task of the lieutenant and his deputies was to raise forces to defend the shire. In some shires the lieutenancy used the pre-civil war assessments as the basis for this work.[80] In the Monson Papers there are estimates for 'common and private armes' for Kesteven and Holland, which could have formed the basis for assessments.[81] It is apparent from a letter of October 1660 that little progress had been made. Just one captain had been appointed and further appointments of commissioned officers would only be made when Lindsey received lists of prospective captains. After the captains had been appointed the task of raising troops from the wapentakes could begin.[82] A note of all the trained bands and volunteers in Lincolnshire survives with a date of 1660. Though there is no information apart from the names of the commanders of the regiments and troops, it is claimed the shire had four regiments of foot with five hundred men in each regiment, six troops of horse with fifty men in each of the troops.[83] It appears unlikely that these militia troops were armed ready for action by the end of the year in the old style dating. In February 1661 there was a report from Kesteven that they had not appointed all their captains for its horse troops.[84] As we shall see, even with statutory authority it took well over a year to assess and raise the militia forces. The 1660 return is probably the number of troops they aimed to raise. In many shires, while the work progressed troops of volunteers were raised for their defence. Lindsey reported in 1660 that Lincolnshire had five volunteer troops with fifty men in each troop.[85]

The 1662 statute gave the lieutenant and his deputies the authority, after an assessment of the real and general property of commissioners, to impose contributions to the militia. Owners of land of a yearly value of £500 or more, or goods or money in excess of £6,000, were to provide a horse and trooper with the required weapons and armour. A minimum of £50 from land or £600 in personal property made a person liable to provide a foot soldier who could either be a pikeman or a musketeer.[86] The cavalry were the most expensive and effective part of the militia. The lieutenant and his deputies were allowed to join together landowners with a minimum of £100 from land or £1,200 in personal wealth to find the costs of a horse and horseman. In the 1663 statute it was stated that no one with a minimum of £200 from land or £2,400 in personal estate was to be charged towards the cost of foot soldiers. The lieutenant and his deputies were also given the discretion to decide whether or not those with land worth between £100 and £200 or personal wealth of £1,200 to £2,400 should be charged for foot or horse.[87] No assessments appear to survive for

80 D. P. Carter, 'The Lancashire Militia 1660–1688', *Transactions of the Historic Society of Lancashire and Cheshire* cxxxii (1983 for 1982), 157–8.
81 LA Monson MS 7/11/71 (an undated list).
82 LA Monson MS 7/12/7.
83 PRO SP 29/27/73.
84 LA Monson MS 7/14/9.
85 PRO SP 29/27/73.
86 14 Charles II c.3, s.ii, iii, iv.
87 14 Charles II c.3, s.iv; OB 42 has the names of landowners in the jurisdiction of Caistor sessions 'joined' to find the cost of a horse.

Lincolnshire[88] but the lieutenant in 1664 reported the number charged for goods was 'not considerable' and generally found in the towns.[89] The 1663 statute authorised the lieutenants to require parish constables to find from their area of jurisdiction the cost of a foot soldier by imposing a levy on those with less than £50 in landed wealth or £60 in personal property.[90] The assessed were not required to serve in person but they had to provide for their substitutes the weapons and equipment specified in the statute, and their pay. In 1663 the rates of pay for a trooper, which had previously been set at 2s a day, were increased to 2s 6d, while the rate of pay for a foot soldier remained at 1s. Lindsey was to complain that no one would serve as a foot soldier for at least 1s 6d a day or 2s. In 1667 the deputies stated that only the statutory pay would be charged.[91] A commission of peers assessed the contributions of the nobility to the horse from their returns of the value of their lands in the shire.[92]

The task of rating and then raising the troops proceeded slowly. It was not until July 1663 that the 530 soldiers charged for the Holland district were summoned to a muster. Only 481 appeared and seven were 'taken to horse' by certificate. No other figures for the Holland regiment, which was commanded by Sir Henry Heron, appear in the letters but they were divided into six companies.[93] It was only in January 1664 that the lieutenant was able to express his 'pleasure' that Sir John Newton's Kesteven regiment was settled and its six companies were complete. By September 1663 there were three regiments, with the third based on Lindsey district under the command of Lord Castleton.[94] Forty-two horse were charged on the Holland district but at the July 1663 muster only thirty-six appeared.[95] In some shires the assessment of the peers' estates led to a substantial increase in horse troops.[96] The commission ordered the Lincolnshire peers to find a total of twenty-four horses. Lindsey ordered eight should be assigned to his son Willoughby's troop; the remainder were to be distributed by the deputies.[97] Maintaining the numbers of horse troops was a continual problem. In January 1664, when only 38 horse appeared for Holland, Lindsey ordered eight horse to be taken from Lord Willoughby's troop and given to Oldfield's troop.[98] In 1664 Lindsey confirmed that there were three regiments of foot, Sir John Newton's, raised in Kesteven, Sir Henry Heron's from Holland and Lord Castleton's from Lindsey. He did not specify the numbers in each regiment but claimed they totalled 2,100 men, which included the Lincoln company of one hundred men. There were six troops of horse with again no indications of the numbers in individual troops, but Lindsey claimed in total they were about 360 men.[99] Numbers

---

[88] M. A. Faraday, *Herefordshire Militia Assessments of 1663* (Camden 4th Ser. x, 1972), shows how assessments could be calculated.

[89] Oxford, Bodl. Clarendon MS 92, fo 144v.

[90] 15 Charles II c.4, s.iv, v.

[91] 14 Charles II c.3, s.v; 15 Charles II c.4, s.ii; PRO SP 29/78/46, 47 are drafts of the letter sent to the shire, see Nottinghamshire Archives DDP 37/3, fos 42r–43r; OB 67.

[92] 14 Charles II c.3, s.xxxii; OB 17.

[93] OB 7, 43.

[94] OB 16.

[95] OB 7.

[96] The Nottinghamshire nobility were to find 42 horse: Nottinghamshire Archives DDP 37/3/21v.

[97] OB 17.

[98] OB 20.

[99] Oxford, Bodl. Clarendon MS 92, fo 143.

in the troops and regiments inevitably fluctuated and no precise figures could be given even after all the troops had done their duty. The deputies explained that no exact figure could be given until all the deputies met in conference. The attendance figures at general meetings, which at their height reached twelve, indicate that this was an unlikely eventuality. After a conference, with the muster master, the deputies 'conceive' the foot to be about two thousand and the horse about three hundred and fifty.[100]

The lieutenant and his deputies had the legal powers to hear appeals against their assessment, to fine men for non-appearance at musters and training and for attendance with defective equipment. The penalties were left to the discretion of the deputies with a statutory permitted maximum of £20 for a horse and troop and for a foot soldier £5. In Lincolnshire arms finders were used to ensure that the men appeared for service with the required equipment and pay. The deputies decided that the finder could, in the case of a default of horse and trooper, be fined 20s a day.[101] Though fines on defaulters were seen by the crown as a possible source of additional funding for the militia, there is no indication in the letters that in Lincolnshire they made even a minor contribution.[102]

There were two challenges which could have undermined the militia assessments, and as a result the effectiveness of the militia. The first came from the unlikely source of 'his majesties best subjects', the volunteers, who had offered their services in the first months of the Restoration, and in 1664 five troops of horse remained as an auxiliary force of about four hundred men. Some volunteers used this service as an excuse to ignore their statutory obligations to the militia. The practice was widespread, for in Kesteven about a hundred volunteers absented themselves from the training, 'many' in Holland followed their example and in Lindsey their actions were cited as a precedent for absence. After the lieutenant had informed his deputies that absences were not to be allowed they tried to enforce the law by levying distresses. Such actions conflicted with the statements of King and Council that every encouragement should be given to the volunteer forces, which were seen by the crown as an important supplement to the militia. Lindsey therefore ordered his lieutenants to cease imposing penalties until he visited the shire. A combination of an appeal to the loyalty of the volunteers, thanks for their services and a reminder of the law and the consequences of absence should have been able to stop the practice. No further report survives of widespread absences by the volunteers. It was, however, necessary in 1666 to remind the volunteers that their service did not exempt them from their militia obligations.[103]

The additional militia statute of 1663 empowered the lieutenant or three of his deputies to order the parish constables to assess by means of a rate men below the minimum financial limits for funding a foot soldier for contributions to the militia. It was such an order that led the constable of Market Deeping to assess, among others, Thomas Bird, a chandler of the town, at 2s 6d. Bird, advised by William Mapletoft, an attorney, sued the constable in the three-week court of the town. The arguments used to prove the illegality of a statutory obligation are not

[100] OB 32.
[101] 14 Charles II c.3, s.viii, ix; 15 Charles II c.4, s.iii; OB 27.
[102] OB 29, 61, 63.
[103] PRO SP 29/27/73; Oxford, Bodl. Clarendon MS 92, fo 143v; OB 26, 31, 32, 33.

known but they were accepted by Hill, the deputy steward of the court, who fined the constable. The deputies who made the order to the constable informed Lindsey of the verdict of the court, claiming that it discouraged the King's officers from enforcing militia obligations in the town. Lindsey, a Privy Councillor, reported the incident to his fellow Councillors, who took swift action to crush this challenge. Bird, Mapletoft and Hill were summoned to appear before the Council on 14 April 1665. On that day the King was also present. Hill, after making his submission, was discharged; Bird and Mapletoft were committed to the Fleet prison, where they remained until their release on 26 April. After such decisive action no more challenges to the deputies' assessments are reported.[104]

THE FINANCES OF THE MILITIA

The 1662 statute established two sources of funding for the militia. 'In times of apparent danger' the crown was permitted, from 25 June 1662 for three years, to raise a sum not exceeding £70,000 a year.[105] The apportionment for each shire was based on the eighteen months assessment granted in 1661, which raised £70,000 a month from England and Wales. The amount to be raised from Lincolnshire was £2,722 4s 10d.[106] The assessments and collection procedures were to be those of the eighteen months assessment. The sums raised were to be paid to the sheriff of the county and distributed on the orders of the King. The statute also permitted the lieutenant to levy from his shire for the 'furnishing of ammunition and other necessaries' an amount which did not exceed in one year a fourth part of the monthly assessment. The assessments, which were to be the same as the monthly and eighteen months assessment, should have raised over £680 a year. To distinguish this levy from the monthly pay, it was often known as the 'weekes tax'. The lieutenant was instructed to appoint a treasurer or treasurer's clerk to receive the weekly pay and distribute it on his orders. According to the statute the official appointed to receive the monies was every six months to account, in writing, to the lieutenant and his deputies, send duplicates of his accounts to the justices of the peace, and certify his accounts to the Council.[107]

The crown ordered the raising of the monthly assessments in all three of the permitted years. John Thornton, the under-sheriff, served as receiver of the three assessments. The sheriffs became the custodians of the money.[108] In August 1663 permission was given for the payment, out of the monthly assessments, of the commissioned officers according to their rank and days of service up to a maximum of fourteen days' service. These sums averaged £231 a year and with salaries of about £30 a year became the major charges on the assessment.[109] As there were substantial surpluses on the assessments their administration and safekeeping were essential. It was not until March 1664 that, on the instructions of the Council and lieutenant, the deputies asked Thornton for his account of the

[104] 15 Charles II c.4, s.iv, v; PRO PC 2/58, fos 45r, 51v, 57r; OB 40, 44.
[105] 14 Charles II c.3, s.xxii.
[106] 13 Charles II St.2, c.3; Oxford, Bodl. Clarendon MS 92, fo 143.
[107] 14 Charles II c.3, s.vi, xi.
[108] OB 2, 22, 36.
[109] OB 8, 15; *CTB 1681–5* ii. 815–16.

first assessment. Thornton was 'under some Surprize' and unable to comply. When he made his account cannot be established but in March 1665 Lindsey asked for the accounts of Sir John Buck, the sheriff for 1662–3, and his successor Sir Edward Dymock. The production of an account for the second levy was delayed by the death of Sir Edward Dymock, the sheriff for 1663–4. Sir Edward Barkham, the sheriff responsible for the third levy, evaded the order of Council and lieutenant for some time and the failure to enforce his compliance made a major contribution to the disappearance of a substantial sum from his account.[110]

In January 1664 Sir John Buck was ordered to transfer the surplus on the first assessment to his successor. Sir John was slow to comply, for it was not until May 1665 that he was expected to be paying in this money. By this time the crown had directed that, for safe keeping, the surpluses should be placed in a chest with its three keys placed in the hands of the lieutenant and two deputies. When he ordered that the chest be kept at Lincoln, Lindsey gave his key to Sir Thomas Meres.[111] The crown, first by suggestion and then by an order of June 1665, instructed the lieutenants to send the surpluses to the Tower of London for safe-keeping.[112] In the next month Sir John Buck paid £4,455 to an officer of the Tower and an additional £200 which came from the first two assessments.[113] Sir Edward Barkham either ignored or evaded the order to dispatch surpluses to London. In July 1666 the lieutenant was asked to certify to the Council the sums of money remaining in the shire and to ensure surpluses were paid to Sir Stephen Fox, paymaster general. This order, which was made shortly before the second Earl's death, was not enforced. In December 1666 his successor, the third Earl, was informed that the order had been ignored and was told to send the money immediately. Eventually £1,000 was conveyed to Fox. It was not until 1681, after an account for all three years with unaccounted arrears of £1,722 0s 4d was presented to the Treasury, that the third Earl was asked for an explanation. He claimed to have little knowledge of monies raised in his father's time and though he was reluctant to trust his memory Lindsey did remember £1,000 being in Barkham's hands. Barkham was held responsible for the bulk of the missing money for it is apparent that there had been an investigation of his estate, which after his death was settled on his son. His widow had remarried a lawyer of the Inner Temple and refused to admit any liability for the money. Lindsey warned that the arrears would only be collected with great difficulty and they remained unpaid.[114] The crown's order to send the surpluses on the monthly pay to London was unpopular, occasionally ignored, and attacked in the House of Commons. It meant that for Lincolnshire over two thirds of the money raised went into the King's coffers. Though about a third of the sum taken from the militias throughout the country was used to defray costs of the militias, in 1666 the majority was used for other military purposes. A substantial sum, which could have been used to meet militia costs in times of emergency, was lost and meant the role of the militia was limited. In 1683 Lindsey remembered that at the time

110 OB 22, 23, 37, 38.
111 OB 36, 37.
112 *CSPD 1664–5*, 395–6, 409, 438, 448–9, 478.
113 PRO SP 29/127/8.
114 *CSPD 1666–7*, 320; *CTB 1681–5* ii. 815–16, 878.

the crown's action caused great dissatisfaction, for the gentry looked upon the monies as appropriated for the militia. The raising of the weekly pay, he informed the treasury commissioners, has 'ever since gone down very heavily'.[115]

In January 1663, when Lindsey sent on the Council's order to raise the first monthly pay, he ordered his deputies to establish the rates for raising the weekly pay. To collect the weekly pay at the same time as the monthly was administratively convenient, as was the appointment of John Thornton, the receiver of the monthly pay, to receive and disburse the money. For 1663–64 Thornton made an account and in 1665 an account was requested by the deputies; whether or not the statutory requirement to account every six months was met is unclear.[116] When Thornton left the treasurership, probably in 1666, no steps were taken to replace him or recover any surpluses in his possession. In June 1667 the urgent need for money uncovered important recent but preventable deficiencies in the administration of the pay. The Holland deputies had failed to inform the lieutenant of the sums raised in their district in 1666. The account for Lindsey was in arrears because monies had been left in the hands of collectors in the wapentakes who were ordered to pay the money at the next quarter sessions. The third Earl of Lindsey continued to delay the appointment of a treasurer and ordered the chief constables of the wapentakes to retain the money raised in 1667 until an appointment was made.[117]

The 1662 statute ordered that the costs of ammunition and other necessaries should be met out of the weekly pay. The 1663 statute added the cost of the inferior, that is non-commissioned, officers to the weekly pay for their fourteen days' duty. The Council ordered the captains of each troop or company to be responsible for their payment.[118] The Lincolnshire deputies, in the sums they authorised Thornton to pay, also added an amount for emergencies so that the captains of the horse received £18 and captains of foot £15. In 1663 £10 was given to the deputies to pay the clerks for their administrative duties.[119] Though there are no surviving accounts for the weekly pay it is apparent that the cost of 'trophies' for the troops were also found from this source. Lindsey reminded his deputies to pay the clerks and also to maintain some reserve for future occasions. The ending of the monthly pay left the weekly pay as the main source of finance for the militia. It was in Lindsey's view a sufficient sum for the annual wages of inferior officers on the fourteen days' service, ammunition and trophies, but it could never be the source of substantial funding for the militia.[120]

---

[115] Western, *Militia*, 45–8; *CTB 1681–5* ii. lvii, 878. Seaward, *Cavalier Parliament*, 238 n.14, argues there was no clear statement in the statute against bringing the money out of the counties and dispensing it nationally. This appears to be so but it is clear that the bulk of the money was not used, as the statute seems to imply, for the militias and this made the demands so unpopular.

[116] OB 2, 26, 37, 47.

[117] OB 60, 63.

[118] 14 Charles II c.3, s.vi; 15 Charles II c.4, s.xiii.

[119] OB 8, 16, 18, 36.

[120] OB 45.

THE TRAINING OF THE MILITIA

An effective militia had to be trained in the use of serviceable weapons. The 1662 statute established procedures for the listing of men at the first muster. Replacements for listed men were allowed only with the permission of the deputies, who had the power to fine unauthorised substitution or absences. It was the task of the arms finders to ensure that soldiers appeared at the musters duty and training with the required arms and pay. The 'finders' could be fined for any defaults.[121] In the 1662 statute a distinction was made between a muster and the training which could be held four times a year. A muster, including travel to the venue, was not to last more than four days; a training was limited to two days. In Lincolnshire it was customary to restrict the time spent in travelling by holding separate musters for each district. The 1663 statute permitted a duty, which was not to exceed fourteen days, to be held as a replacement for the muster and training. The crown seized the opportunity presented by the legislation to order that one twentieth of a shire's militia be constantly kept on guard. It was claimed the duties would be the most effectual way of preserving the peace. There were restrictions on the duty, for no man was to serve for more than fourteen days, and except in an emergency the winter months and harvest were to be exempt from duty.[122]

Lindsey ordered the foot regiments to stand guard at Lincoln where the militia store was kept. The deputies organised the roster which began on 15 October 1663 with a company from Castleton's regiment. After the companies of the Lindsey regiment had completed their duty they were to be followed by the company of Sir John Newton's regiment and finally companies from Heron's regiment, until all had completed their duty by 21 July 1664. During the two winter months, when the companies were on duty, the Lincoln Company of Sir John Meres was to guard the magazine 'by proportion'. The Council accepted that in most counties a twentieth of the horse troops would be too small a number to be an effective force. The horse were to be reserved for emergencies and not placed on duty until the end of the first period of July. It was not until May 1664 that the deputies ordered their horse troops to do their duty. Three troops were to journey to Lincoln, two to do duty at Grantham while Oldfield's troop served their duty at Sleaford.[123] Three deputies took the opportunity of the duty to inspect Oldfield's troop, which was found to be 'well horst' and in all other respects complete, with some minor defects which could be left to Sir Anthony to remedy. In their report on the first year of duty the deputies informed Lindsey the duties had been completed without disorder or disturbance and the soldiers by exercising were rendered 'very use full'.[124]

It was not until March 1665 that Lindsey ordered preparation for the next fourteen days' duty to be made. The duty, with the exception of the companies ordered to go to Lincoln, should have begun on 5 April. On a plea from the deputies that frost and snow had delayed the sowing it was postponed until May. Two

---

[121] 14 Charles II c.3, s.xxiv.
[122] 14 Charles II c.3, s.xx; 15 Charles II c.4, s.viii.
[123] OB 18, 16, 26.
[124] OB 30, 32.

important changes were ordered by Lindsey. Though a minority of the companies were to mount guard at Lincoln, the majority were assigned to the main ports, which were nearer their homes. The foot companies were to be divided into two sections with each undertaking seven days of duty.[125] To keep the foot troops together for seven days would give an opportunity for more intensive instruction than a muster or training. The lieutenant and his deputies believed the duties to be of considerable benefit to their troops. Lindsey reported that by exercising for fourteen days his soldiers had become 'good firemen and fitt for service'. There were, as the Holland deputies implicitly admitted, limits to what could be achieved by one duty. In 1665 they asked for permission to take their companies on route marches, for though they have 'learnt their discipline' they did 'not as yet well know how to march'.[126]

THE MILITIA IN ACTION

The militia had two main duties: the maintenance of order, and the defence of the realm against rebellion and invasion. The first was essentially a police function, at a time when even the most basic duties of law enforcement were often beyond the limited abilities of parish and hundred constables. The second was a military responsibility when, as a result of opposition to a standing army, there were only a small number of regular army troops available to the crown.

The task of the militia was to defend the restored monarchy and its supporters' control of the country. On the orders of the Council it disarmed former members of the Protectorate and Republican forces. In 1662 searches were given statutory authority, provided the constable was amongst those ordered to take the arms of those judged dangerous to the peace of the kingdom. As the Lincolnshire militia was desperately short of arms, Lindsey asked his deputies to report how many of the weapons could be used for the King's service and where they were stored. After the first surge of activity it was not until June 1664 that Lindsey ordered the arms should be sent from various parts of the shire to the store at Lincoln.[127]

The news of the Yorkshire rising led to Sir John Monson's troop being placed on guard at Lincoln for a week and Lord Willoughby's troop summoned to Grantham. The deputies sent one suspect under guard to the sheriff of Yorkshire, and the confessions they had taken from others under suspicion.[128] It was not until the summer of 1665 that there was widespread activity against those in Lincolnshire judged to be a danger to the crown. The rumours of plots by the 'phanatiques' to overthrow the crown led to orders to imprison the most dangerous and take bonds for their good behaviour from men judged to present a lower risk. The Oldfield papers have a list of men summoned to attend quarter sessions and the stipulations of their undertaking to remain at peace with the King and his subjects. The alleged leaders were sent to Lincoln jail in an opera-

---

[125] OB 37, 39, 43.
[126] Oxford, Bodl. Clarendon MS 92, fo 143v; OB 43. The training of the troops should have been led by the muster master. 15 Charles II c.4, s.vi ordered that he should be paid from contributions of his soldiers. There is only one mention and no identification of the holder of this office (OB 32).
[127] PRO SP 29/8/188; 14 Charles II c.3, s.xiii; OB 1, 26, 28, 29; LA Monson MS 7/11/20; 7/12/17.
[128] Oxford, Bodl. Clarendon MS 92, fo 143r; *CSPD 1663–4*, 323, 440.

tion in which at least thirteen deputies from all parts of the shire participated.[129] The imprisonment of Colonel Edward King of Ashby de la Launde achieved a wider significance for it brought into question the legality of these proceedings. Oldfield and Sir Robert Carr sent militia troops with a summons for King to appear before them at Sleaford. Though King had been a leading Parliamentarian soldier who fell into dispute with the Lincolnshire county committee by 1659, he was seen as a potential supporter of the monarchy and protested he had actively supported the Restoration. King, who claimed he was summoned because Carr had a grudge against him, refused to enter a bond of £2,000 for his good behaviour, for such terms, he believed, were 'illegal, infamous and servile'. As a result of his refusal he was imprisoned in the common jail of Lincoln. He was later to claim that after he had read the mittimus he offered security for his good behaviour, which was refused. When King demanded his writ of habeus corpus his challenge threatened to bring into question the legal validity of not only the proceedings against him but all such imprisonments. He successfully secured his release but in January 1666 was summoned to appear before the Council with the jailer of Lincoln who had allowed him his freedom in advance of the legal proceedings. At the Council meeting, at which Charles was present, King refused to give security for his good behaviour and was imprisoned in the Tower. After his release he stood in 1667 against Sir Henry Belasyse, a deputy lieutenant, at a by-election for Grimsby. Shortly after his defeat King left the shire.[130]

Disorder and riots among the lower orders usually brought decisive action from those who ruled. In Lincolnshire reactions to the riotous actions against Fen drainage could be fractured by the support some gentry had for their own and the commoners' rights. The first Earl of Lindsey and Sir John Monson were among the leading projectors who stood to benefit substantially from drainage projects. They were supported by the King and the law courts, and assisted by unscrupulous manipulation of the membership of the commissions of the sewers. At various times the justices, sheriff and occasionally the militia were ordered to take action to protect the drainage works and their workmen.[131] During the civil war the commoners took the opportunity to ruin many of the works. The Rump and Protectorate regimes also favoured the projectors and on one occasion Major General Whalley used troops to suppress riots. In April 1663 enclosure began at Wildmore Fen, where 4,000 acres had been granted to the crown. The commoners replied by indictments of the workmen at Horncastle sessions for riotous entry and unlawful enclosure. The crown's response was to remind the justices and sheriff of orders from the House of Lords for their quiet possession of the Fen. Sir Edward Dymock, the sheriff who was also a deputy and justice, was ordered to enforce the order and Robert Peake was sent to supervise the work. Dymock's family had previously supported the commoners and it was later claimed his son 'countenanced the rioters'. The disturbances of 6–7 August 1663, which destroyed fences and houses, and saw assaults on workmen, were the subject of Peake's report to the Council with a list of the alleged main partici-

[129] Nottinghamshire Archives DDP 37/3/88v; OB 46; PRO SP 29/134/13.

[130] PRO SP 29/135/123; 133/4; 148/113; 150/108; PC 2/58, fos. 323, 343; C. Holmes, 'Colonel King and Lincolnshire Politics, 1642–1646', *Historical Journal* xvi (1973), 451–84; *House of Commons 1660–1690* ii. 682–4.

[131] Lindley, *Fenland Riots*, 15, 51–5, 66–8, 72–5, 139–62, 181–3; *CSPD 1663–4*, 219.

pants. Peake also reported that Dymock took no action, an inactivity which led to a rebuke from the Council. The Council ordered Lindsey to suppress any further unlawful assemblies and tumultuous insurrection. The lieutenant sent the direction to his deputies with a plea for the utmost vigilance. Whether the vigilance led to reports and action is unclear. In 1664, when there were further attempts to enclose, it is significant that troops were sent to restore order. The use of militiamen, many of whom would be from the Fens and have a natural affinity with the commoners, was, in the particular circumstances of Lincolnshire, a risky enterprise.[132]

It was the sectaries who gave Oldfield the greatest concern. In 1664 Lindsey reported there were three to four hundred Quakers, Anabaptists and other sectaries in his shire, the majority in the Isle of Axholme or in the Marsh.[133] Oldfield reported a concentration of sectaries around Spalding, increased on occasions by men and women from the adjoining shires. In May 1664 he complained their 'poyson' was spreading so quickly that they outnumbered those who stood firm for King and Church and they were infiltrating the militia.[134] It was their often confrontational behaviour and contempt for social hierarchy that made the Quakers appear particularly subversive. The oaths of allegiance and supremacy were regarded as the test of loyalty. The Quakers' refusal to take these or any oath was an indication of their potential disloyalty. The 'Sufferings', the Lincolnshire Quaker records of their prosecution, show that in the years 1660–63 their meetings were disrupted by 'swordsmen' and Friends imprisoned for their refusal to take the oaths. An incident reported in the Sufferings also helps to explain why Oldfield and other justices were so determined to attack the Quakers. Early in 1663, after a meeting at Gedney was dispersed, on the orders of a justice, its leaders were sent to Spalding jail. Here they were visited by other Friends who, when they were refused permission to enter the jail, stood outside the window listening to the exhortations from the imprisoned. The crowd only dispersed when Oldfield arrived with constables and soldiers and arrests were made. It was the refusal of the Quakers arrested at a meeting to plead before Oldfield and the justices at Kirton sessions that led Sir Anthony to insist that the oaths be put. He is recorded by the Quakers as saying 'if we let them alone they will trouble us this Sunday and the next'. It was claimed these oaths were not formally put but still imprisonment resulted and they remained in jail, as they were not called to quarter sessions.[135]

Oldfield's letters show the difficulties the Lincolnshire authorities had in dealing with the Quakers. In July 1663 he asked Lindsey how they should proceed, for the jails were full and too small to take the sectaries, and he suggested a military course should be taken. In May 1664 the lieutenant claimed that, by reason of the checks they had been given and the constant pressure on them, the sectaries had become more modest, less frequent, than before. Neither the Sufferings nor Oldfield's letters have any record of increased activity in the

---

[132] OB 11–14; Lindley, *Fenland Riots*, 146, 161, 224–7.
[133] Oxford, Bodl. Clarendon MS 92, fo 143; R. W. Ambler, *Churches, Chapels and the Parish Communities of Lincolnshire 1660–1900* (Lincoln, 2000), 30–36.
[134] OB 6, 24, 25.
[135] LA Soc. Fr. 1&13, pp. 61, 69, 71–74; B. Reay, 'The authorities and early Restoration Quakerism', *Journal of Ecclesiastical History* xxxiv (1983), 69–84.

preceding year. In the next month Sir Anthony was reporting an upsurge of sectarian activity. He also indicated the limitations of the legislative attempts to control the Quakers. The Quaker Act stipulated three months imprisonment for refusal to pay a fine for the first offence of refusing to take the oath and six months for a second offence. The Quakers served the term of imprisonment and sued for release. Particularly infuriating for Oldfield were the acquittals by the assize judges.[136] A determination to make the law more effective by imposing penalties for sectarian meetings led to the Conventicle Act of 1664. It encouraged lieutenants and deputies to dissolve or prevent conventicles and take persons they found at these gatherings into custody. Though the Sufferings for 1665 record an upsurge in imprisonments, the majority of which were for being present at conventicles, neither they nor the Oldfield letters refer to activity by the militia. Oldfield maintained his hostility to the Quakers and used their refusal to give bonds for their peaceable behaviour and undertakings not to attend religious meetings as an opportunity for imprisonment.[137]

In the allocation of militia responsibilities it had become the practice to distinguish between maritime and inland shires. As Lincolnshire was a maritime shire, the Lincolnshire deputies were instructed to assist the Vice Admiral in the pressing of seafaring men for naval service.[138] During the second Anglo-Dutch war Lincolnshire's coastal trade was often attacked and its havens and estuaries seen as possible landing places for an invasion. The length of the country's coast made adequate coverage by the militia an impossibility. After the warning of an invasion in January 1666 Lindsey and his deputies followed the order of the Council and placed the militia on guard at or near the ports and estuaries that were most likely to see a landing by the enemy. From their six locations the horse troops had the potential to respond quickly to any incursions. The foot regiments were given a wider, essentially watching brief. The Kesteven and Holland regiments, with their headquarters at Boston, were to guard the coast from Wainfleet southwards; the coast northwards from Wainfleet was the responsibility of the Lindsey foot, who were to be quartered at Louth. It was left to the deputies to decide on the location of the 'outguards', as they should find best from time to time.[139] Vital to any response would be the watch kept and the warnings sent by the fires lit in the coastal and inland beacons. The beacons were a long established warning system but many were in urgent need of repair and furnishing with the necessary flax and pitch. The effectiveness of the detailed orders of 8 February for the maintenance and watch from the beacons depended on surveyors who were to be appointed by the chief constables of the wapentakes.[140] The emergency lasted for about three weeks before the troops were discharged from their duties. After the sea battles against the Dutch in early June the lieutenants were ordered to ensure their militias were ready for action. As the emphasis in the order was to avoid 'expense and trouble at the time of harvest', the militias were instructed to be ready at an hour's notice to repair to their colours at the locations

---

[136] OB 6, 24, 25; Oxford, Bodl. Clarendon MS 92, fo 143; 14 Charles c.1.
[137] 16 Charles II c.4, s.v, viii; LA Soc. Fr. 1&13, pp. 82–86.
[138] OB 35.
[139] OB 48, 49; this alert was caused by news of the preparations of the French fleet; Seaward, *Cavalier Parliament*, 238.
[140] Boynton, *Elizabethan Militia*, 132–6; OB 50.

assigned in January. The deputies were to ensure that a strict watch be kept from
the beacons by the hiring of six able and honest men to keep the watch. There
were frequent attacks on shipping along the Lincolnshire coast and the Humber
in July. After two ships off Wainfleet were driven ashore, Boston raised volunteers to defend the port and their town. The offshore alarms did not result in the
majority of the militia forces being placed on duty before 6 August when the
Council judged the threat of invasion had passed.[141] During the July emergency
the crown had asked the Earl of Lindsey and two other peers to raise three regiments of horse of about five hundred men, to be paid from the surpluses of the
monthly tax. The regiments and other horse troops and a foot regiment raised at
this time were stood down in September but were ordered to remain ready for a
recall, which came in the next year. In the summer of 1666 these forces could
provide a more immediate response than the militias and were to be sent to the
areas at most risk from invasion. These independent forces have been described
as a 'select militia' and it has been suggested that they could have been the
making of the militia. This is to misinterpret their purpose. The crown viewed
these forces as a temporary expedient. Though they were paid out of the monthly
tax, no attempt was made to establish this as a permanent source of funding and it
was quickly used for other purposes. These forces were not meant to, and did not,
solve the problems of defending the shires and how such defence should be
funded.[142]

In May 1667 information that the Dutch fleet was about to sail led the Council
to order the militias to be on alert and the beacons made ready and watches kept.
If the enemy landed the militias were instructed to make the largest show of horse
they could find, even if they included horse otherwise 'unfitt and improper' for
service, for their numbers would discourage any landings.[143] The news that the
Dutch fleet had appeared off the Kentish coast led Lindsey to order his forces to
travel to such places where there was the 'greatest apprehension of danger'. The
deployment of their forces with some changes of venue followed the pattern of
the previous year. The most important development was to give each of the foot
regiments a part of the coast to defend and some companies were specifically
assigned to the defence of coastal towns and havens. The lieutenancy decided, by
the addition of volunteers, to increase the horse troops to eighty and asked for
permission to raise more volunteers and as a last resort to raise the shire by the
posse comitatus.[144] The warrants ordering the raising of the militia on the orders
of the lieutenant and his deputies mentioned fourteen days' pay and the service
was treated as if it was a duty lasting for the fourteen days permitted by statute.
However the fourteen days' duty was, by the 1663 statute, specifically limited to
three years.[145] The crown had, in the 1662 statute, a way of securing the active
services of the militias in case of invasions, insurrections or rebellions. Those
liable to serve or find soldiers were to serve or provide pay for no more than one
month. If this was done provision was to be made for repayment out of the

[141] OB 51, 52; *CSPD 1665–6*, 517, 550; *CSPD 1666–7*, 65, 76.
[142] *CSPD 1665–6*, 454, 475–6, 489; *CSPD 1666–7*, 166–7, 176; *CSPD 1667*, 172, 179–83, 189; BL
Add. MS 34,222, fos 54v–55r; Western, *Militia*, 45–6.
[143] OB 58.
[144] OB 62, 63.
[145] 15 Charles II c.4, s.viii.

crown's revenues and no one who made a financial contribution was to be charged again until they had been repaid. In its letter of 25 June, though the crown mentioned the invasion of the Dutch, it did not enforce the statutory requirement, for it was admitted that there was no money to pay the militias and other troops.[146] The crown was in such a desperate need of funds that it asked the lieutenants, deputies, justices and chief gentry to consider how the militia should be funded and promised to find all due means and ways for reparation and satisfaction. After this request and the plea for a loan, the shire replied that they were exhausted by taxes and no ready money was available.[147] The deputies did not propose to leave the shire unguarded. All they could provide in July was a guard of two foot companies, one at Grimsby, the second at Burgh le Marsh, and a horse troop at Wainfleet which it was admitted would only be effective against 'little incursions'. They asked that the adjacent inland counties, whose militias were discharged, be ordered to send soldiers. In the event of an actual invasion the gentry did offer to find in addition to the shire's forces a 'considerable proportion' of horse for six weeks. They also deflected the request for a loan by placing the onus on the crown.[148]

'A militia transformed' was Professor Fletcher's verdict on the Restoration militias.[149] His survey praised the institutional efficiencies of the militias and argued that the weekly pay provided a permanent fiscal basis for its work. Central to his argument is a comparison with the pre-civil war militias, a comparison which cannot, in the absence of sufficient evidence, be made for Lincolnshire. The Oldfield letters cover the majority of the years when militia activity was at its height. The letters throw most light on the work in the Holland district but they do show that there was a core of deputies in the shire who took the duties seriously and could be relied on during emergencies. There were important administrative defects. The administration of the finances of the militia became lax, it left the weekly tax without a treasurer and led to the disappearance of a substantial sum of money from the third monthly assessment. In Lincolnshire the size of the shire and the resulting organisation of the militia inevitably led to decentralisation. General meetings of deputies from all three districts were necessary to prevent conflicting or partial decisions being made and for a coherent county-wide response. Though there were attempts to organise general meetings to coincide with the assizes these did not become a permanent feature of the administrative calendar. When these were held, even a small majority of the deputies was rarely achieved. General meetings, as the years 1666 and 1667 demonstrate, could be quickly arranged and deputies responded speedily to the emergencies. Such responses were one of the main strengths of the militia but these were constrained by the funding and concept of the militia. A golden opportunity to establish a sound financial basis disappeared when the substantial surpluses of the monthly assessment were taken out of the shire, for the weekly pay was sufficient to pay only for the yearly costs of ammunition, the wages of non-commissioned officers and some incidentals such as trophies. Against invasion the crown had the right to

[146] 14 Charles II c.3, s.vi; OB 64.
[147] OB 64, 66, 67, 70; *CSPD 1666–7*, 43. For a similar explanation for Nottinghamshire's reluctance to contribute, see Nottingham University Library Pw 1/129; Seaward, *Cavalier Parliament*, 240–44.
[148] OB 66, 70.
[149] Fletcher, *Reform in the Provinces*, 316–32.

use the militia for a month, provided it was able to repay these costs, but in 1667 dire financial difficulties deterred ministers from making use of these powers. The militia could be effective in the discharge of police duties as it rounded up suspects and occasionally raided conventicles. Against a rising it was unlikely that the twentieth of the foot on duty could have had an impact unless the challenge was in close proximity to its guard station. To guard even the main estuaries and ports from invasion could only be maintained in the short time span of the fourteen day duty. At best the militia could provide a very limited response and this was how its role was perceived. The opportunity to expand the militia's activities was lost when the crown took its financial potential. The Oldfield letters show the impact of this decision and how it restricted the militia's role.

TAXATION AND LOCAL GOVERNMENT

In Appendix One there are eight documents which illustrate other important aspects of local administration in Lincolnshire. The assessment and collection of taxation was under the supervision of men appointed by Parliament. In January 1662 Oldfield, as sheriff, was appointed general receiver for Lincolnshire of the eighteen months assessment granted by Parliament in December 1661. The assessments, an efficient direct tax established after the first civil war, were repeatedly used in the first years of the Restoration. The amount to be raised in England and Wales was decided by Parliament, then divided amongst the shires according to their presumed wealth. The county commissioners, appointed by Parliament, imposed on their shires a pound rate which would raise the required monthly amount. Nationally £70,000 was to be raised each month, of which Lincolnshire was to find £2,722 4s 10d. The assessment became the source of funding for the militia. The three monthly levies for the militia and the weekly pay used the established systems for assessment and collection.[150]

In 1663 Parliament decided to revert to subsidies, the customary method of raising taxation before the civil war. As a result of under-valuation the yields of the subsidies had suffered substantial decline. The letter of the Council to the county commissioners, who included Oldfield, tried to ensure that the valuations would produce sufficient revenue for the King's 'pressing occasions'. Though the report of the meeting of the Lincolnshire commissioners appears to have accepted the Council's instructions, an addendum to the general distributive scheme nullified its impact. In their assessment of the value of real property the commissioners were permitted to take into account debts and other necessary expenses and allowed comparisons with former subsidies. Sir Philip Warwick, the Secretary to the Treasury, described the subsidy as 'a most ridiculous tax' and its yield was so disappointing that Parliament reverted to the assessments.[151] In 1667 a poll tax attempted to meet the criticism that the assessments were unfair to landowners by taxing the 'more elusive forms of personality', particularly the income from money and offices. The reports in the Oldfield letters show the

[150] OB 74; C. D. Chandaman, *The English Public Revenue 1660–1688* (Oxford, 1975), 140–43, 157, 170–75; M. J. Braddick, *Parliamentary Taxation in Seventeenth Century England: local administration and response* (London, 1994), 126–50, 158–67.

[151] OB 75, 76; Chandaman, *Public Revenue*, 145, 149–50, 157; 15 Charles II c.9, s.v (p. 461).

commencement of the work of the commissioners for the rating and assessment of the poll tax.[152]

The one new tax of these years was the Hearth Tax. In 1666, when its collection was put out to farm, William Batt became the sub-farmer for Lincolnshire and Edward Copley his collector. The agreement (Document 80) is an attempt by the justices and farmer to find a solution to disputes which in many shires disrupted the collection of the tax, particularly with the constables who remained responsible for collection in the parishes. As no records of the Holland quarter sessions are extant after the Restoration until 1674, we cannot investigate the work of the justices of the peace.[153] The record of a quarter sessions at which Oldfield presided shows that, as usual, responsibility for the repair of the highway remained a burden and had to be enforced by the order of the justices.[154]

ECCLESIASTICAL DISPUTES IN SPALDING

The restoration of the episcopal church was seen by many as an essential part of the re-establishment of the political and social order. The Lincolnshire militia showed their public approval of its return by firing volleys in honour of Robert Sanderson, Bishop of Lincoln, when he appeared in the shire to begin his visitation.[155] Yet, as the letters show, there were disputes between the clergy and men who were their supporters.[156] In their defence the clergy were to claim that only 'severe proceedings' could remedy the neglect of their ecclesiastical courts. Oldfield was reported to have been excommunicated; his offence is not specified in the correspondence but it could have arisen out of a dispute about tithes. Sir Anthony complained about the proceedings to the Earl of Lindsey, who informed the King. The lieutenant was instructed by the monarch to acquaint the Archbishop of Canterbury with Oldfield's grievance. Lindsey's advice to Oldfield was to let the proceedings take their course.[157] Sir Anthony remained a firm supporter of the Church. As his letters demonstrate, he led the opposition to Robert Peirson, rector of Spalding, a man of 'factious principles' in the 'factious town of Spalding'.

Peirson had succeeded Robert Ram as rector of Spalding.[158] According to the articles presented against Peirson, he soon showed his opposition to infant baptism and god-parents. He was to assert the validity of presbyterian ordination and was a member of a gathered church. It was also claimed that he had refused to support the Lincolnshire petition for a freely elected Parliament. The divisions

---

[152] OB 77, 78, 79; Chandaman, *Public Revenue*, 146–7, 163–4, 157, 180–1; Braddick, *Parliamentary Taxation*, 233–40; 18/19 Charles II c.1.

[153] OB 80; Braddick, *Parliamentary Taxation*, 241–70; Chandaman, *Public Revenue*, 88–109.

[154] OB 81.

[155] *Mercurius Publicus* (1662 no. 29), 462.

[156] As OB 82 shows, Oldfield did attempt to defend a clergyman.

[157] OB 19, 21; J. Miller, *After the Civil Wars: English politics and government in the reign of Charles II* (Harlow, 2000), 138; CUL Dd.ix. 43, pp. 22–3 is a record of tithe dispute and disagreement about repair of the chancel between John Oldfield and Robert Ram, which occurred before Ram left his cure in 1656. The document has as its heading 'January 28 1664 about tythes'. No court proceedings about this case appear to survive. The document has not been transcribed.

[158] W. Shaw, *A History of the English Church during the Civil Wars and under the Commonwealth* (2 vols, London, 1900), ii. 325, 536, 590; Firth and Rait, *Acts and Ordinances* ii. 981.

in his church and the town became clear in 1660 when he refused to use the prayer book presented to him by one of his churchwardens and ignored the recently erected baptismal font. Under the leadership of Oldfield a plea was made to the Bishop that Peirson not be licensed, for he would not conform to the liturgy and discipline of the Church and he had not been episcopally ordained.[159] According to the Act of Uniformity, or Conformity as Oldfield described the statute, Peirson had to pass three tests. By 17 August, the Sunday before St Bartholomew's Day, an incumbent had to read morning and evening prayers from the recently revised prayer book and to make a public declaration of 'unfeigned assent and consent' to all it contained. Before the Ordinary of the diocese he had to subscribe declarations repudiating the Solemn League and Covenant and the taking up of arms against the King. If an incumbent was not episcopally ordained he was required to receive such ordination.[160]

A survey of the diocese of Canterbury has demonstrated the difficulties of enforcing the legislation and the inadequacy of the tests for detecting partial conformity.[161] Peirson met one of the tests when he received ordination from Thomas Sydserf, a Scottish bishop who became Bishop of Orkney. He apparently made the required declarations before Sir Edward Lake, Chancellor of the Lincoln diocese, and was granted a licence.[162] In his conduct of the services at Spalding, and his continuing opposition to the sacrament of infant baptism, it was clear that Peirson was ignoring the declarations about the validity of the prayer book. When he was challenged on these issues Peirson's explanation that he had 'subscribed and declared to the use of the Lyturgy not the Doctrine therein contained . . .' clearly did not amount to unfeigned consent. It is clear from Oldfield's correspondence that Pierson had a 'considerable' following in the parish, which in 1662 included the support of the churchwardens and some of the feoffees. The problem for Sir Anthony was how to remove, in the terminology of Bishop Sanderson, such a 'hollow hearted subscriber'. Oldfield and his supporters collected and listed Pierson's many offences against the canons of the church but the effectiveness of this approach was not tested. The issue was settled and potentially prolonged litigation avoided when Peirson resigned his living.[163]

EDITORIAL METHODS

The manuscript has been transcribed with abbreviations usually extended and the original spelling retained. The spelling of words and occasionally names can vary within the same letter; these differences have been retained.

The original headings of the letters in the manuscripts have been retained. Where they are incomplete or headings are missing the editor's headings are shown in square brackets.

---

[159] OB 83, 85.
[160] 14 Charles II c.4, s.ii, iii.
[161] I. M. Green, *The Re-Establishment of the Church of England 1660–1663* (Oxford, 1978), 143–77.
[162] OB 83, 84, 85; Green, *Re-Establishment*, 151; *DNB* xix. 255.
[163] Green, *Re-Establishment*, 149; OB 84, 85, 86.

The documents are arranged in three sections: militia affairs, taxation and local government, and ecclesiastical disputes at Spalding. In these sections the documents have, with the exception of OB 42, been arranged in chronological order. The very few undated manuscripts are placed according to their position in the manuscripts. New style dating has been used.

THE LETTER BOOK OF
SIR ANTHONY OLDFIELD

THE LINCOLNSHIRE MILITIA

1. [The Earl of Lindsey to the Deputy Lieutenants]

To the Right Honourable Robert Lord Willoughby, etc

Having received Informacon that Divers Armes late in the Custodie of Disaffected persons have been secured by severall Officers and soldiers under my Command in the county of Lincolne, I do therefore desire you will be informed in whose hands they are and the certaine number of them and how many of them fixed armes, that they may be disposed of for his Majesties service and in the mean time that you will take care that they be not imp=berelled but safely kept in whose hands they are now in, till you have further order from

Your affectionate friend
Lindsey

West(minster), 13[1]

[p. 18]
[1] Apart from '13' the letter is undated.

2. [The Earl of Lindsey to the Deputy Lieutenants, 13 January 1663][1]

Wheras I have Received His Majesties Command the 19 of December[2] last past forthwith to raise or order my Deputyes within my Lieutenancy to raise a Monthes Assessment after the rate of 70 thousand per mensem in pursuance of the Act for Ordering of the forces in the severall Counties of this Kingdome, for the defraying of the Militia,[3] His Majestie judges it necessary to be imployed till the 25 day of June next ensuing. These are therefore to appoint you forthwith to put into Execution all and singular his Majesties commands and more particularly expressed in a Transcript thereof which I have here sent you. And whereas by the late Act of Parliament[4] you or any three or more of you are impowered to lay fiting rates within my Lieutenancy not exceeding in the whole in any one year the proportion of a fourth parte of one monthes assessment after the rate of £70 thousand per Mensem for furnishing Ammunition and other necessaryes, which I conceive requisite to be put into Execution and you are to direct that the sayd monyes soe levied and collected bee paid unto John Thornton of Hornecastle in the County of Lincolne gent. whome in Pursuance of the said Act I have appointed Treasurer for Receiving and paying the same. And when other moneyes shall or may accrew by the power given you by the said Act to such Orders and Directions as he shall from time to time Receive from my selfe or from any three of you; I bid you heartily farewell

Your affectionate friend
Lindsey

Whythall 13

[pp. 20–21]
[1] The letter, apart from '13', is undated but, as OB 3 shows, it was written on 13 January.
[2] A copy of the transcript can be found in BL Add. MS 34306, fo 23rv.
[3] 14 Charles II c.3, s.xxii.
[4] 14 Charles II c.3, s.vi.

3. To Sir Anthony Oldfield at his house at Spalding

Sir Anthony

Bee pleased to accquaint Sir William Trollop with the Inclosed; the like is taken with the rest of the Deputy Lieutenants in Kesteven and Lindsey. I desire you will send my Lord as soon as you can an account of the Values of the Peeres estates in Holland which were returned by the Commissioners; soe remaines

Your most humble servant
Edward Christian[1]

Westminster, 13 January 1663
I opened this Edward Christian

[p. 21]
[1] Christian was Lindsey's secretary.

4. To Sir William Trollop at[1]

and Worthy Sir[2]

I received this Inclosed the 20 at 8 of the Clocke in the night and I here send you the Individuall paper as they came to my hand; would you would please to favour me with your transcription in this concerne, and that I may have your leave and to set your hand and Sir William Thorolds hand, for you well know I am alone, for I desire to doe the same what you doe, for I am soe environd with terrors of destruction (as much as lyes the power of water) soe that it is allmost alltogther impossible for me to waite you in person.

Spalding   Anthony Oldfield

[pp. 21–22]
[1] The manuscript is blank. Trollop's house was at Casewick.
[2] The initial part of the address is erased.

5. To Mr Edward Christian

Mr Christian

In Obedience to your Lords Commands I accquainted Sir Edward Barkham about the having the Holland Troop; he rejoyced to here of my Lords favour to him, and said, he would endeaver to serve the King under my Lord to the uttmost of his life and fortunes. We have a muster the Seaven and twentyth of this instant at Kirton, but noe body to Receive the Horse; if you please to remind my Lord of it and if my Lords good pleasure continue still towards him, perhaps he may either send him a Commission or a letter to Receive them for the present. I am jealous the Bostoners will make but a slender appearance with their foot; I went on purpose to Bourne to get some of those Deputy Lieutenants that were there for the fourteenth day where I found Sir ffrancis ffaine, Sir William Trollop and Sir Robert Markham with a well becoming appearance both of Horse and Foot. I had as many of them promised me as I shall not need to fear but that our meeting will hould at Kirton the 27th, at Surfleet the 28th and at Spalding the nine and twentyth at present. I have no more to say but to begg of you not to forget my most humble duty to my good Lord

Your friend and servant
Anthony Oldfeild

Spalding, July 17 1663

Postscript

When I was at Bourne I was speaking to Sir ffrancis ffaine that I wondered some of the Gent would appeare soe farr as to put it to a dispute for one (if I did not mistake) that had served the Rebells more especially when one of my Lord Lieutennants servants had the right to it, I nameing you he replied, why had he any right to it, I told him yes, he said, they have then injured me for I protest, to God, I did not know of any Compeditor Leaving had, I would have doubly paused before I would have set my hand where Mr Christian was concerned. This he was pleased to say to me, and as for myselfe you shall alwayes find me that I am

Your true friend
Anthony Oldfeild

[p. 40]

6. To the Right Honourable the Earle of Lindsey, Lord Great Chamberlaine of England at Westminster

Haist Haist
For His Majesties Service

To My Lord of Lindsey

May it please your Lordship

I judge it my duty to His Majesties service and my obligation to your Lordship to accquaint you that severall iniurious meetings are held here abouts, by severall persons who come out of other Countryes, their principles are dangerous and their numbers considerable enough to give apprehension of dangers. In severall Companyes they goe up and downe in eight or nine score in a Company in the compasse of half a score miles. I have with other Justices proseeded according to the late Act against some of the heads of them yet they groe like Hydrayes and the rest continue their meetings in contempt of His Majesties Lawes and Authority, and therfore I humbly begg your Lordships Directions how to proseed for the Goales are two little to hould them, soe that some military course be applyed either to punish them or prevent their groeing mischiefs which may arise from men of their Tenents.

Spalding, 17 July 1663

Your most humble and faithfull Servant always to be commanded
Anthony Oldfeild

[pp. 43–44]

7. From Sir William Trollop, Sir William Thorold and Sir Anthony Oldfeild to my Lord of Lindsey

My Lord,

In pursuance of your Lorships commands we have lysted and sworne both Horse and ffoot in these parts of Holland, we have used (we thinke) all possible diligence in the setling the forces and more particularly begg leave to tell your lordship of those that deserved the best, which was the Bostoners, that your Lordship may please to encourage them if you think fitt, the particular accounts are these written, and of all occurrences we shall give your Lordship speedy and continuall accompts and with all readines put such other orders in Execution as your Lordship shall please to send to

My Lord
Your Lordships most humble and obedient Servants
William Trollop, William Thorold, Anthony Oldfeild.

Spalding, July 29 1663

Charged	530 Foot
Appeared	481
Non Appeared	049
Taken of to Horse by certificate	007

Charged	042 Horse
Appeared	036
Non Appeared	006

[p. 41]

8. [The Earl of Lindsey to the Deputy Lieutenants, 12 August 1663][1]

By the Inclosed which is a Transcript of the Directions I lately received from the Lords of his Majesties most Honorable Privy Counsell, taking into their consideration the late Act Intituled an Additionall Act for the better ordering of the fforces in the severall counties of this Kingdom, and have thought fitt againe to recommend to my care the speedy and effectuall establishment of the Militia in my Lieutenancy for preserveing the Peace of the Kingdome besides the Instructions I formerly received, have thought it necessary to quicken the dispatch and to mind me of some of the particulars expressed in the said Act, not doubting of the more then ordinary care and sircumspection in all the matters aforesaid, have given me the further occation to desire you will use all the possible care and diliegence in setling the Militia within my Lieutenancy, that according to the powers and directions given it may be of more use to his Majesties service; to which I have so much experience of your good inclinations as assures me I shall not need to add more then which is his Majesties pleasure, yet nevertheless since that at present I have no opportunity of conferring with you I shall give my opinion that Lincolne is the most convenient place to keep the Magazine and the body of ffoot together in that are to be on duty, that incouragement be given to the Commission Officers and charge allsoe duly to discipline and instruct their Souldiers whilest they are uppon that Service and keep them in good order and that you have an inspection over them and wheras his Majestie hath made an establishment of pay for the Commission Officers to be paid out of the 70 thousand pounds when they are uppon dutie and have appointed the Serjeants, Corporalls, Drums, Trumpeters and other inferior Officers to be paid out of the weekes assessment I desire you will prepare an establishment for the same and other necessaryes to the respective Componyes and Troopes and when I come to the Country (which I intend shortly) I may together with you further advise which may be necessary and in the meane time if you think fitt to send out your Warrant

for the weekes assessment for this present year I leave to your good directions
and bid you heartily farewell

Your affectionate friend
Lindsey

Westminster, 12 August 1663

[p. 42]
1   The letter, apart from an 'M', has no heading.

9. To my Lord of Lindsey from Sir ffrancis ffaine, Sir Thomas Monson etc (17 August 1663)

My Lord,

Having newly Received a letter from your Lordship of the fifte of this instant[1]
with Instructions from the Lords of his Majesties most Honourable Privy
Counsell directed to your Lordship that we shall with all delligence and industry
obey your Commands in order to the securing of the Peace of this County, and in
all things else observe your Directions, but though we are now in readiness for
present duty wee humbly desire (by your Lordships favour that Harvest being
now begun) we may forbeare the drawing our men into actuall duty until the end
of Harvest, unlesse there appeare some cause of danger here to us or we Receive
some further orders from your Lordship and so we rest

Your Lordships most humble Servants

Francis ffaine	Thomas[2] Monson
Thomas Hussey	William Trollop
Robert Markham	William Thorold
Anthony Oldfeild	William Wray
Edward Rossetor	Charles Pelham

Lincolne, August 17 1663.

[p. 43]
1   PRO SP 29/78/46, 47. The Council's letter, dated 5 August.
2   A transcription error for John.

10. To Mr Edward Christian[1]

My very good friend

I received yours and its Hansh = en= kelder[2] Clustered with Commands, my
duty shall not be taskd to perswade my obedience to the performance of them. I
have send you what you writ for the Estates of the Peers in Holland.[3] I have taken
(or rather in truth given me) two three handed swords which was and are my
Lords; 'tis my beleife you never laid your eyes on such; King Arthurs Table
would make a buckler paralell for bulke, Antiquity and value; convey my duty in
such humble regards as you may thinke fit to my Lord.

Yours etc
Anthony Oldfeild

[p. 44]
1   The letter is undated.
2   Hans in kelder, or womb (OED).
3   Cf. OB 3, 17.

11. To the Kings Most Excellent Majesty and to the Lords of his Majesties Most Honourable Privy Counsell. The Humble Petition of Richard Peeke Gent imployed by your Majesties Surveyor Generall as an agent for your Majesty in Wildmore ffenn in Lincolnshire.

Humbly showeth,

That the Lords in Parliament have lately made severall orders for the quieting your Majesties possession of Wildmore ffenn as it was in the year 1641 and that the Sherriff, under Sherriff [and] Justices of the Peace of the Countie aforesaid should appease all Ryots that should any wise happen about the same and prevent the throwing down of Ditches Mounds and ffences of the said ffenn; and that in case of disturbance therein the said Sherriff and Justices ot two or more of them should commit the Malefactors to the Common Goale.

That your Majestie by your Letters of the 22 July last directed to the Sherriff of the said County recommending the Execution of the said Orders to the Sherriff.

That the Severall persons named in the schedule hereunto annexed with others to the number of two or 300 Horsemen and ffootmen uppon the 6,7 days of this instant August being assembled in a Ryotous and Tumultuous manner in your Majesties part of the said ffenn with force and Armes threw down your Majesties part of the fenn, pulled downe a house there belonging to your Majestie and burnt the Materialls thereof and all the moveable goods that where therein, beate and wounded Charles Newby, George Melbourne Jun and Oliver Swann Inhabitants in the said House.

That some of the said Ryotors continued their meetings and took sheets and made flags and one Captain Hart, one of their leaders (who was one that Petitioned your Majesties Royall ffather to Judgement) encouraged his fellow ryoters and said stand to me my boyes for we were never in a ffayrer way if we can but levie money ennough.

That the said orders of Parliament and Letter were delivered to the said Sherriff and afterwards he, being informed by your Petitioner that the said Ryoters were assembled and acting as before is set forth, came to the place, found them soe acting and being there desired by your Petitioner to use his Authoritie for the quieting your Majesties possession and suppressing the said Ryot according to the said Orders and your Majesties Letter did utterly refuse to doe the same but went away whereby the said Ryots were much heightened in their Actings.

Your Petitioner therfore conceiving himself in duty bound to give an accompt thereof to your Majesty and your Counsell doth humbly submit the Examination and Punishment of the offenders as to your Majesty in your Princely wisdome shall seeme most agreeable for the preservation of your Majesties Peace and the Early suppression of such Tumults least they prove the fore runners of great mischiefs

And you petitioner as in duty bound shall dayly pray etc
Concordat cum Originali

Richard Browne
Theophilus Hart
John Thornehill of Marum with his sword
John Richardson of Cunsby

Edward Pond of Tumby
Robert Middleborough of Langworth
Thomas Brumley of Cunsby
Richard Bray of same; Samuel Wall of same
Richard Clarke of Whyte houp
Joesph Marryot of ffishtoft
Christopher Turugton of Cunsby
Francis Tillson of ffordbanke
John Smeaton of Cunsby
William Middlebrough of Langworth
Robert Cawthorpe of Marum
John Wright of Kearsby
Richard Tippin of Cunsby; William Hardy of the same
Luis Pie of Rearsby
Richard Simpson of the same
John Walker
Amos Walker
Allin Towle

Concordat   Richard Browne

[pp. 45–46]

12. To our very Good Lord the Earle of Lindsey, Lord High Chamberlaine of England and Lord Lieutennant of the County of Lincolne

After our hearty Commendations to your Lordship we send you herewith the Coppie of a Petition exhibited at this board touching a Ryotous and Tumultuous Assemble (of very dangerous consequence) in Wildmore ffenn within your Lieutennancy on that part thereof which is sett out for his Majestie and the names of some principall persons therein and we have sent the like to the high Sherriff of the County of Lincolne requireing his answer in writing to that part thereof wherein he is concerned and have sent a Serjeant at Armes for Captain Hart (who headed the Ryot) and John Turnehill, Richard Clarke and Richard Bray who countenanced, assisted and encouraged the same, we have thought fitt to accquaint your Lordship herewith recommending to your vigilant eye and circumspect care the prevention and suppresseing any further inconveniences which may arise by such unlawful Assemblies and Tumultuous Insurrections which are commonly forerunners of greater mischeifs that soe the Peace of the Nation may be happily preserved, we are well assured of your Lordships ready compliance and best endeavers therin and bid your Lordship very heartily farewell from the Court at Whythall this 19 day of August 1663.

Your Lordship very Loving friends

Clarendon	Thomas Southampton	Angelsey	Sandwich
Albermarle	St Albans	Bath	Thomas Wentworth
Barkshire	Middleton	William Compton	Charles Berkeley
Gilbert London	John Berkely	Henry Bennet	George Carteret
Ashley	William Morrice	Richard Brown	

[p. 47]

13. To the Right Honourable George Viscount Castleton, Robert Lord Willughby of Earsby and the rest of the Deputy Lieutennants.

By the enclosed which is a transcript of the letter of Directions I Recevied from the Lords of His Majesties most Honourable Privy Counsell dated from the Court at Whtehall the 19 of this instant August together with a coppie of a Petition exhibited to the Counsell board touching a Ryotous and Tumultuous Assembly in Wildmore fenn within my Lieutennancy and their Lords have recommended to my care the preventing and the suppresseing any further inconveniences which may arise by such unlawful Assembles and Tummultuous Insurrections which are comonly forerunners of greater mischiefs that so the Peace of the nation may be happily preserved. I desire therefore your immediate vigilency Circumspection and care touching the same, whereby I may give his Majestie a good account of what is required of

Your affectionate friend

Lindsey

Wytham, 22 August 1663

[p. 48]

14. To the Right Honourable the Earle of Lindsey Lord Great Chamberlaine of England, Lord Lieutennant of the County of Lincolne.

My Lord,

By especiall order and Command of his Majesties Counsell I here Inclosed send you the coppie of a Letter directed from the Lords of his Majesties most Honourable Privy Counsell unto the Sheriffs of the Respective Countyes, to the end that your Lordship may the better know what you are to expect and require from the Sheriff of your County and Precinct of whose due performance according to the tenure of the said Directions and to your satisffaction as his duty obligeth. Not doubting, I rest

Your Lordships

Most humble servant

Richard Browne

Whytehall, 4th September 1663.

Copia Vera.

[p. 51]

15. [The Privy Council to the Sheriffs, 2 September 1663]

After our hearty Commendations, These are to let you know that notwithstanding his Majesties Incomperable Clemencie to persons disaffected to his Government they have not hitherto desisted from ploting and contriveing new mischeifs against the same, in their frequent Assembles dangerous meetings and Conventicles in many places of the Kingdome, wherby we are in prudence oblieged to applies all remedies that may prevent those evill which such practices may draw uppon this Nation; And amongst others by ordering the Milita into such a posture as may be most useful to that purpose; one part wherof is to give all encouragement that may be to the Officers as well as the Souldiers of the Trayned Bands by paying such as shall doe duty for the time they are imployed therin. Wherefore you are herby required to pay out of such moneys as you have Received out of the Monthes Tax of Seaventy thousand pounds heretofore Levied on the Nation by Vertue of the late Act Intituled an Act for Ordering the fforces of the severall Countyes of this Kingdome to such person or persons as the Lord Lieutenant for the County and his Deputyes or any three or more of them shall appoint. It being for the payment of ffourteen dayes pay in the year to the Commission Officers of Horse and ffoot from a Captain Inclusive downewards, if soe much duty be by them done within the time aforesaid (viz) to a Captaine of Horse p.diem ten shillings, to a Lieutenant of Horse six shillings to a Cornet ffive shillings, to a Quartermaster of Horse four shillings per Diem, to a Captain of ffote per diem eight shillings, to a Lieutenant ffour shillings, to an Ensigne three shillings per Diem; and the Receipt of the Persons or persons to whome you shall pay those monyes by the order aforesaid shall be unto you a good ample and sufficient discharge for soe muche as you shall pay. Not doubting your punctuall performance hereof we bid you heartily farewell from the Court at Whythall this Second day of September 1663

Your very loving friend
Richard Browne

Copia Vera

[p. 52]

16. [Resolutions of a meeting of the Deputy Lieutenants 8 September 1663]

Lincolne, 8 September 1663

Resolved; That the High Sheriffe by himself or Deputy doe pay to all the Superior Officers upon duty according to Establishment which is as followeth (viz) A Captain of Horse 10/- per Diem, A Lieutennant of Horse 6/-, To a Cornet 5/-, To a Quartermaster 4/-, To a Captain of ffoot 8/-, to a Lieutennant of ffoot 4/-, To an Ensigne 3/-. And this for 14 dayes at any time when they shall be so longe upon duty signified under the hands of two or more of the Deputy Lieutennants and the Recepit of the Captain to be a discharge for the mony.

Resolved; That the Tresurer of the weekes pay shall pay unto the Superior Officers for 3 Sarjeants for the time they shall be upon duty xviii pence per diem for every of them for three Drummers xviii pence per diem for every Corporall xiiii per diem.

Resolved; That the Treasurer of the weekes pay shall pay unto two Trumpetters of each Troop 3/- per diem and unto 3 Corporalls 3s per diem.

Resolved; That a Constant Guard of ffoot be uppon duty at Lincolne 14 dayes every year, the ffirst Company to begin the 15th of October next and the Lord Castletons Regiment shall begin his duty and continue it untill all the Companys in the Regiment hath done duty.

Resolved; That after the Lord Castletons Regiment Sir John Newtons Regiment shall releive Lord Castletons Regiment according to the former Resolves. And that Sir Henry Herons Regiment shall relieve Sir John Newtons Regiment according to the former Resolve.

Resolved; That Sir Thomas Meeres Company be reserved to Guard the Magazine by proportions the two months the other forces doo not duty.

Resolved; A Generall Meeting be the 15 of October 1663.

[p. 55]

17. To the Right Honorable George Viscount Castleton, Robert Lord Willughby of Earsby [and] the rest of the Deputy Lieutennants for the County of Lincolne

Wheras the Lords Commissioners appointed by His Majestie have in pursuance of the Act of Parliament for Ordering the fforces in the severall Counties of this Kingdom Assessed and charged the Peeres estate who have made returns of the yearly values there of within my Lieutenanncie in the County of Lincolne and have Respectively Certified the same by me that I may take effectual care that the Horses charged may be in readines uppon all occations for his Majesties Service, I have therefore by my letters accquainted the Respective Peeres therwith that the same may be provided with such Armes offensive and Defensive with the furniture for the Horses as by the said Act is directed which I doe not doubt but they have given directions to their Bayliffs or Tennents to take care of, the number of which Horses soe Respectivelly Charged I have heer unto annexed. And I would have those Horses charged upon my selfe to be added to my Sonne Willughbys Troope, and the rest you may add to the other Troops as you shall find most convenient. Since I have had noe returns (notwithstanding my severall Letters) of the yearely value of my Lord Standhops Estate, I am required to certifie to your returne therof, which I desire you to make to me, with what convenient Speed you can. My Lord Willughby of Parchams Estate being lately sold is not charged by the Lords Commissioners but left to be charged by you. I have herewith sent you a Coppie of the Letters from the Counsell Board to the Sherriffs of this Respective Countyes for payment of the monies assigned by his Majestie for the Commission Officers whilst they are uppon duty that accordingly you may give Order touching the same as occation requires; soe not doubting of your Vigilancie and care in all things that may concerne his Majesties service I remaine

Your affectionate friend
Lindsey

Wytham, 15 September 1663

Poste

I received your Letter dated the 8th Instant and am well satisfied with your proceedings and you being uppon the place what you thinkest where the Magazine shall be I shall approve of, and when the King is gone from these parts I shall send Christian back to London, and then he will take care to provide the Ammunition and send it to Boston by Sea if I here nothing from you to the contrary.

Lindsey

The number of Horses charged uppon the Peeres Estates in the County of Lincolne

The Duke of Buckingham	Two Horses
The Earl of Lindsey lord lieutennant of the county	Eight Horses

The Earl of Lincolne	ffour Horses
The Earle of Exciter	Three Horses
The Earl of Moulgrave	One Horse
The Earl of Cardigan	One Horse
The Lord Bellassis	One Horse
The Lord Dacres	One Horse
The Earl of Stamford and his Lady	halfe a Horse ⎱ joyned
The Lord Peters	halfe a Horse ⎰
Elizabeth Countesse Dowager of Exeter	halfe a Horse ⎱ joyned
The Lord Brookes halfe a horse	halfe a Horse ⎰
The Lord Viscount Campden	One Horse

[pp. 53–54]

18. [Resolutions of the Deputy Lieutenants, 9 December 1663]

Linconle, December 9th 1663

Resolved; That Mr John Thornton Treasurer for the weekes Assessment, Doe pay Annually to every Captain of Horse And Foot soe much as shall make up what he hath or shall Receive; the sum of ffiftteen pounds to every Captain of ffoot, the sum of ffifteen pounds to every Captain of ffoot and eighteen to every Captain of Horse out of the weekly Assessment for his yeares duty for the satisffaction of under Officers and other Emergencies for which the Captains Certificates shall be his Discharge.

Resolved; Allsoe that the said John Thornton doe pay into some of the Deputy Lieutennants hands of every Sessions the summe of Ten Pounds out of the weekes Assessment by them to be distributed amongst their Clarkes that hath taken paines in setling the milita in pursuance of Directions which we have lately Received from our Lord Lieutennant the Right Honourable the Earle of Lindsey, and the said deputie Liuetennants Receipts shall be his Discharge.

John Monson. Thomas Hussey. John Newton. Edward Rosseter. Thomas Meeres.

[p. 56]

19. [Edward Christian to Sir Anthony Oldfield, 31 December 1663]

Sir Anthony

I received yours of the 14 Instant and must beg your pardon that I did not returne you an answer sooner. I am very sorrie their was any mistake concerning the last General meeting of the Deputy Lieutennants at Lincolne whereby you lost your Labor. The Information I gave you of the time was uppon a letter I Received from Sir Thomas Meres dated the 12 of November who by it ceritifies that their next Generall meeting was appointed that day the Month after and by that accompt the 10 of December was the time apppointed. I have likewise advice that the next meeting is to be on the 20 of January. I presented my Lord with your Letter to me concerning the severe proceedings of the Churchmen which his Lordship shewed to the King and after his Majestie had perused it expressed his dislike of the proceedings and commanded my Lord to accquaint the Bishop of Canterbury with it, which his Lordship has done, and you will find the fruits of it, but his Lordship would not have you take any notice of the business but let it worke it Selfe, in the meane time some say they have no other way for those that neglect their Courts and will not pay their dues and that your selfe were excommunicated by them. I thank you for your kindnes to my Sister Watson but she is advised not to send any more to Mr Burton but that he send his mony to Mr Thornton and uppon payment of it and the Law charges he will see that their shall be a Discharge given and if he will not I perceive their will more charges run and Mr Burton may thanke himself for delaying soe long; soe take leave to subscribe

Your most humble servant

Edward Christian

Westminster, 31 December 1663

My Lord is making way that you may have his horses added to your Troop about Brigg end as most Convenient.

[pp. 58–59]

20. [The Earl of Lindsey to the Deputy Lieutenants of Kesteven and Holland, 23 January 1664]

ffor the Deputy Lieutennants acting in the parts of Kesteven and Holland in the Countie of Lincolne

Gentlemen I received yours of the 13th of the instant from Sleaford which inclosed Lysts of the Horses Charged in Kesteven and Holland as you have divided them into three Troopes and since their are but 38 Horses raised in Holland for Sir Anthony Oldfeilds Troop I would have eight horses about Brigg end taken of my Sone Willughbys Troop to be added to them. I should be glad these three Troopes were fuller, and doe not doubt but it may be done when you have further consulted it. I shall not particularize my observation on the Lysts but committ them and the returnes made by the Constables to your Reviewe hopeing you may find out wherin his Majesties service may be advanced without puting the extremity of the Act. I am very glad you have setled Sir John Newtons Regiment that the Companies may be compleate when they come upon the Guards. So I rest

Your affectionate friend

Lindsey

Westminster, 23 January 1664.

[p. 57]

21. [Edward Christian to Sir Anthony Oldfield, 25 January 1664]

Sir Anthony,

You have extended your favour to me soe largely that I am soe much in your debt I know not how to get out of it but you may be confident I am obliged, soe serve you in which lyes in my power. Your Letter to me I had the opportunity to read to my Lord when the partie was present which suggested the Excommunication. I can assure you his Lordship is very well satisfied in your concerne. He hath written a Letter to the Deputy Lieutennants acting in Kesteven and Holland a

Coppie wherof I have sent you.[1] In answear[2] to theirs from Sleaford dated the 13 of this instant I can assure you he is well satisfied in your proceedings in Holland but touching the charge of Horse in Kesteven he hopes they will give him a better accompt both in regard of some informations he hath had and allsoe by his own observations on the Lysts sent to him. I must acknowledge my selfe

Your obliged humble servant
Edward Christian

Westminster, January 25 1664

[pp. 57–58]
[1] Cf. OB 19.
[2] In the margin is written 'the letter above is it', i.e. OB 20.

22. To our Right Trusty and Right well beloved Counsell and Counsellor Montague Earle of Lindsey, Great Chamberlaine of England and our Lieutenant of our County.

Charles Rex

Right Trusty and welbeloved Couzen and Counsellor we greet you well. Wheras in the Act for ordering the fforces in the Severall Counties of our Kingdome it is provided that incase of apparant danger to the Government it may and shall be lawfull for us to cause to be levied such summe or summes of mony during the Space of three years from the 25 day of June 1662 not exceeding the summe of seventy thousand pounds for one whole yeare for the defraying the whole or suche parte of the Militia as we shall find our selfe oblieged to imploy in order to the quiet and Security of this Nation. Pursuance to which we did with the advice of our privie Counsell the last yeare send Letters to the Respective Lieutenants and their Deputies to cause the aforesaid summe or summes to be raised in their severall Counties being = thereunto moved by the apparent danger in which the Government was by the plots and conspircies of some unquiet Spirits who had designed the Subvertion thereof, and finding by the experience of one year more that the notority and apparency of the same danger is infintely multiplyed by the restless and never to be satisfied minds of those upon whome the pardon of past offences hath had noe effect then to give them a confidence to commit new ones, and observing the Direction and apprehension under which good Subjects suffer from these disorders being alarmed at home and discouraged abroad in the Execution of those dutyes they owe the publique together with the continuall vexaton and cost they are dayly exposed unto by a necessity of assembling and drawing together the Militia for their Security against the aforesaid Conspiraces and continuances. Now for the better security and ease in the ffuture and for the maintenance of the Publique Peace we have by the advice of our Counsel[1] resolved the issuing forth our Second Letter and doe hereby in pursuance of the said Act charge and command you forthwith to raise or according to the Statue order the Deputies to raise within your Lieutennancy One monthes Assessment after the rate of £70 thousand pounds a month for the defraying such parte of the Milita as we either at present imploy or shall hereafter judg necessary to be imployed and in raysing therof you and your Deputies are exactly to follow and observe such Rules and Directions as are given and expressed in an Act of Parliament for the raiseing of the 18 Months Assessment after the rate of 70 thousand pounds a Month directing that the said mony be soe levied before the 25th day of June next ensuing the date hereof and paid into the hands of the high Sherriff of that our County or Countie; within your Lieutenancy thereto be by him or them kept together with what other monies are yet remaining uppon the Collection of the last yeare in the hands of his or their predecessors or Predecessors the last Sheriff or Sheriffes or any the Collectors which are hereby Authorized and required to deliver the same with him or them with whome our pleasure is, that it continue untill by our Warrant he or they be ordered to disburse it for the use aforesaid and for no other whatsoever, likewise our will and pleasure is that you forthwith Certfie us what and how any parte of the aforesaid Collected Summe of the last yeare have been disbursed or if any omission or defect shall have happened in the passing or issueing forth thereof that you cause a strict enquiry to be made thereupon in the which the high Sheriff together with the respective high Collectors and Receivers are to be answerable with these our Letters shall be unto you and your Deputies as likewise the high Sherriff of that our County the Collectors and Receivers and all others Respectively a sufficient Warrant.

Given at our Court at Whythall the 29th day of January 1664 in the 15th yeare by his Majesties Command

William Morrice

[pp. 25–26]

[1] The transcriber has in error written County for Counsell.

23. [The Deputy Lieutenants to the Earl of Lindsey, 15 March 1664]

To the Righte Honorable the Earle of Lindsey, Lord Great Chamberlaine of England, Lord Lieutennant of the County of Lincolne.

In obedience to his Majesties Commands signified to us by your Lordship for the Levieing of the Monethes Assessment and upon yours for the levieing the 4th parte of an Assessment we have at a Generall meeting agreed our Warrants to issue out for the levying of the same within the time directed and have called uppon Mr John Thornton the late under Sherriff for his accompts for what has been Received and Disbursed by him that we might assigne his Surplasage of the Monethes Assessment as by his Majestie is directed to the under sherriff but finding him under some Surprize we have given him time till ffryday 7 night for the Perfecting his accompts which we shall present to you Lordship as soon as finished

My Lord

Your lordships most humble Servants

John Munson	Thomas Hussey
William Trollop	William Thorold
Robert Markham	Anthony Oldfeild
John Newton	John Walpoole
Henry Heron	John Munson

Lincolne, March 15 1664

[p. 59]

24. Henry Burrell, Anthony Oldfeild, John Jay, Anthony Oldfeild to the Earl of Lindsey

May it please your Lordship

The full expectations we had of an additional Act of Parliament concerning the Quakers, Anabaptists and Sectories in generall, did cause us to be less early in our addresses to your Lordship then otherwise we should have been. The poyson of these dangerous factions doth so spreed itself in these parts as amongst the middle sort of people they of this Judgment out number those that stand firme in their duties to the King and Church; they are such dangerous Seducers as they draw severall even of the Milita themselves to their tenents, who within a few monthes were as opposite to them in Judgment as any men living. Should we return your Lordship a Lyst of those desperate people we must trouble your Lordship with the names of halfe the Inhabitants here; we have therefore at present made onely a Returne of some of their principall (as they call them teachers) and shall further waite your Lordships Commands. None of the Vermin the Quakers excepted refuse the oath of alegeance, which we Constantly tender them; we have formerly filled the Goales with them but at severall Assizes they have been accquitted to the lessening of our Authorityes. We thought it our duties to signife thus much to your Lordship finding these people numerous and desperate in their resolutions then we conceave can consist with the safety of these part; their meetings are Soe full that our Churches are empty. According to your Lordships Commands we shall give all dutiful and readie observance and humbly crave leave to Subscribe

  My Lord

    Your Lordships most humble and faithfull servantes all wayes to
    be commanded

      Henry Burrell, Anthony Oldfeild
      John Jay   Anthony Oldfeild

Spalding, May 16 1664

In obedience to my Lord Great Chamberlaines and Lord Lieutenants Commands we have sent to him to this effect.

[p. 61]

25. To the Right Honorable the Earle of Lindsey, Lord Great Chamberlaine of England, and Lord Lieutenant of the County of Lincolne

May it please your Lordshipp,

We judge it our bounden duty to his Majesties service and our obligation of to your Lordship, to accquaint you that all manner of Sectories (excepting the Papists for we have not one of them in our Country) doe associate and combine even to danger; their numbers too considerable and doe give Suspition of apparent mischeifes. These be the name of the Principall ring Leaders, Robert Addison, Edmund Pettis Preaching, George Grubb of Whaploade, John Yates of Moulton, John Kirkby of Moul., Robert Greeneld, John Horseman, Richard Berch of Spalding, William Drury of Whap., Thomas Bordman a Stranger, John Woodford of Moul., Oliver Oteland, Jess Messe of Whap., Jo Oram, Robert Holdworth, Nathaniel Turpin, Thomas Baker of Whaploade, James Wallet of Wh., Joh Burgate of Wh., Michael Hollings of Moul., Math. Glen of Moul., Jo

Glens Sone of Cowbet, Thomas Cooke, Richard Right of Holbech, Wm Taylor of Gosbertowne, Tho Philips of Holbech, Wm Clarke of Weston, Math. Glen of Moul., William Clarke of Weston, Richard Whale of Pinchbecke, Thomas Ingram, Jo Harrison of Holbech, Jo Rufford of Moul., Richard Bettison de Moul., Thomas Clarke de Moul., Robert Harper de Moul., Thomas Groome de Moulton, Richard Neston de Holbeach, Thomas Browne of Moul., Lawrence Moul of Whap., Edward Prudmore of Moul., John Woodsell and James Dawson, which makes the many severall well grounded imaginations of abundance of men that loves the King take if for granted that if some speedy course be not taken with them, who to speake lesse then their number is full halfe and halfe of them turned, lesse then within this twelve months even many of the Militia, severall letters we have Received from honest men in the Country; for us to take a Course with them [1] we must make or Application to your Lordship for they do say [1] their insolency is soe great) that if they be Suffered to run on they must leave their habitations. And some of them are so dareingly bould as to say it is or will be shortly their Militia. We have continually lyned the Goales with the heades of them but still either the Judges at Assizes or the Act for the three months or six[2] takes them off; the oath of Allegiance they says Tis that that gives them all their Lyberties therfore some few of the Anabaptists will take that. And of Sundays they travell to their Severall Sortes of meetings as if they were to great ffaires; for the only regulation of which we humbly and heartily begg with all our Soules your Lordships Directions how to proceed that we may the better avoid these growing mischeifs that will inevitably arise from them

> My Lord
> > Your Lordships most humble servant allways to be comanded
> > Anthony Oldfeild
> > John Jay, Anthony Oldfeild Henry Burrell

Spalding, May 16 1664
In obedience to the Lord Chancellors Commands we have the done the like to him

[p. 60]
[1] Words crossed out and unreadable.
[2] 14 Charles II c.1. In 'the Quaker Act', non-payment of fines for the first offence of refusing to take the oath was punished with three months' imprisonment, the second offence with sixth months' imprisonment.

26. [Resolutions of the Lord Lieutenant and his Deputies, 24 May 1664]

London, May 24 1664

Montague Earle of Lindsey Lord Lieutennant of the County of Lincolne together with divers of his Deputy Lieutenants resolved

1   That the Armes seized at severall times be bought into the Magazine at Lincolne.

2   That the Distresses on the Volunteers be forborne till your Lordship comeing into the County for their not appearing with their Armes charged to the militia.

3   That a Duplicate of the Treasurers accompts for the Weekes Assessment be returned to his Lordship.

4   That the Milita fforces be all brought upon their duty at the Guard within the year ending 25 of July next.

In order thereto
    That warrants be issued forth to the rest of Collonel Henry Herons Regiment to succeed his owne company uppon the Guards as followeth.

Lieutenant Colonel Thory and Major Ogar to
come Uppon the Guard at Lincoln on the 9 of June 1664 for 14 dayes duty

Captain Booth and Captain Spooner   23 June for the like

Captain Oldfeild and Pickering   7 July for the like

The like warrants be issued forth for the Horse

The Lord Willoughbyes Troop	9 of June at Grantham
Captain Tyrwits	16 of June at Lincolne for the like
Captain Thorold	23 of June at Grantham for the like
Captain Bolls	30 of June at Lincolne for the like
Sir Anthony Oldfeild	7 of July at Sleaford for the like
Sir John Munson	14 of July for 1 week at Lincolne[1]

Wherby all the Guards of Horse and ffoot will end the 21 of July 1664.

[p. 62]
[1] Monson's troop was given one week's duty for they had served for seven days at Lincoln in October 1663 (BL Clarendon MS 92, fo 143).

27. Resolved at a Generall meeting At Lincolne this 17 of June 1664

1   Resolved that the severall Captains of Horse doe keep their Troopes in constant duty and good Dyscipline in the places appointed them reddy for further Service.

2   That all Armes seized by any person in this Lieutennency for his Majesties service are brought within one Month next to the Magazine at Lincolne and Delivered to the Store Keeper who is to repay the reasonable charges of bringing them to Lincolne.

3   That the Magazine at Lincolne be repaired and Secured according to Directions uppon view taken by us this day.

4   That every Armes finder shall be fined 20/- a day for every Horse and Horseman charged on him making default.

[p. 63]

28. [The Deputy Lieutenants to Sir Henry Heron]

Lincolne, June the 17 the 1664
To Sir Henry Heron

Sir. Having received an order from our Lord Lieutenant that the Armes already seized of or that shall be seized on for his Majesties Service be brought and delivered into his Majesties Magzine at Lincolne there to be Secured for his Majesties Service you are therefore to accquaint your Severall Captains and other Officers with the said Order and we require you and them within one month after the date hereof to send In all armes already Seised and all other Armes within a month after the seizure and the Keeper of the Store there have order to repay the resonable charges of bringing such Armes to Lincolne. Dated at a Generall meeting at Lincolne this 17 day of June anno domini 1664.

Ffrancis ffane; William Wray; William Trollop; Anthony Oldfeild; John Newton; Thomas Meres.

[p. 63]

29. [The Deputy Lieutenants to the Earl of Lindsey][1]

To the Right Honourable the Earle of Lindsey
My Lord,
    We received your Lordships Letter of the Second of June and according mett this day at Lincolne and have and will make such inspection of the Horse Guards that they may be in as good Order and Discipline as the ffoot. We have likewise taken care by our Letters to the Severall Collonells of ffoot to be communicated to their Captains as likewise to the severall Captains of Horse as well of the trayned Bands as Volunteers to be communicated to their Inferior Officers to send into the Magazine at Lincolne all such Armes as hath been seized or shall hereafter be seized by them for His Majesties service. What effect this produceth we shall from time to time give your Lordship an accompt off. We have viewed the magazine and find the Ammunition in good Order and have given Order for mending the defects in the Howse which when repaired will be very fit for that purpose. We have likewise given order for the meeting of the other Troopes at the times and places appointed by your Lordship and have agreed uppon fineing defaults both of Horse and ffoot and we have appointed the next Generall meeting at the Assizes which will be about a Month hence when or before we shall be ready to Receive and Obey your Lordships further commandes as becometh
                    Your Lordships humble Servants
                        ffrancis ffaine, William Thorold, William Trollop
                        Anthony Oldfeild, John Newton, William Wray
                        Thomas Meres
[p. 64]
[1] This letter is undated.

30. To the Right Honorable The Earle of Lindsey

My Lord,
    In order to his Majesties Service and in obedience to your Lordshipps Commands wee mett this day where Sir Anthony Oldfeilds Troop of Horse marched in uppon their 14 dayes duty which troop we find to be well horst and in all other respects compleate some defects that which when the Captain gives in shall be taken order in. Those soldiers that had not taken the oath according to the Act of Parliament we have administred to them: At Lincolne Assizes we have

appointed our next Generall meeting were we shall be ready to Receive your Lordships further commands as becometh

Your Lordships most humble and obedient servants
ffrancis ffaine, William Thorold, Thomas Meres

Sleaford, 7 of July 1664

[pp. 64–65]

31. [The Lord Lieutenant to the Deputy Lieutenants]

To the Right Honourable George Viscount Castleton, Robert Lord Willughby of Earsby and the rest of the Deputy Lieutenants of the County of Lincolne

Gentlemen,

I conceive that when the Duty of the whole year is over you will certify me thereof to which I desire you will anex the number of Horse and ffoot within my Lieutenancy together with the names of the Commission Officers in the respective Militia Troopes and Companies that I may present them to His Majesty. I have had yet no accompt of the makeing up of Captain Thorolds Troop. I doe not know how it comes to be lesse then the old Lyst, It is not intended by me that the Milita fforces should be lessened by the Volunteeres, yet in respect of the encouragement his Majesty hath comanded to be given to them I doe desire you Will suspend any proseedings that may seeme sevare to them till my coming into the Country which if my health permit me will be before the Assizes when I hope with you to find out some expedient that may be convenient for all. In the meane time I doe desire that you would let me have a particular accompt a parte drawne up of the horse and ffoot which is wanting by reason of the Volunteers. The Treasurers accompt for the Weekes Assessment is not yet comed to me which I desire may be sent

Your affectionate ffreind
Lindsey

Wytham, 15 July 1664

[p. 65]

32. [The Deputy Lieutenants to the Lord Lieutenant]

To my Lord Lyndsey[1]

Lincolne, August 1664

My Lord, In obedience to your Comands wee humbly returne your Lorship this accompt to your last letter. That for our militia it hath performed the 14 days duty for the last year without any disturbances or disorder And that the Souldiers are by excertiseing rendered very use full. Ffor the Assessment for the fourth part of a Month we sent your Lordship a Duplicate of it; if it hath not miscarried, but if it hath we shall immediately present you with another. Concerning the Volunteers lessening the Traine Bands by lysting themselves we have no abatement in Lindsey but in Kesteven there are about a hundred ffreehoulders taken from the Militia by it and the Captain and officers of the Volunteer horse and in Holland many others fall off upon the same accompt and by this president they claime the same advantage in Lyndsy. Concerning the numbers in the milita as they now stand and charged both Horse and ffoot we can give no exact accompt of it till all the Deputy Lieutenants meet. But upon conference with the Muster Master we conceive the ffoot to be about two thousand and the Horse to be about three hundred and ffifty. ffor the names of all the Commisoned officers we here present your Lordship with a lyst of them, which is all but that we are

My Lord

Your most humble and obedient servant

Willughby	Castleton
Robert Markham	John Monson
Anthony Oldfeild	William Hickman
Henry Heron	Charles Pellum
Thomas Meres	Edward Rossiter
William Ray	Henry ffynes

[p. 66]

1 Apart from to 'my Lord Lindsey', which is at the bottom of the letter, there is no heading.

33.[1]

My servant brought me a Coppie of the Deputy Lieutennants Letter from Lincolne; for I could not go to my Lord of Lindsey and they was pleased to put my hand to it, pray tell my Lord I doe not assert it neither would I set my hand to such a letter which doth discourage his Majesties best Subjects and my Lords Servants the Volunteeres; Lykelyhood and your owne knowledge all most conclude that. In Kesteven the two Troopes of Volunteers Sir Christophers was made up could not account to   2 Taken off of a hundred freehoulders[3]

[p. 67]

1 The letter is without date or heading, but refers to the issues discussed in OB 32.
2 The words here are crossed out and unreadable.
3 The transcript ends.

34. [The Lord Lieutenant to the Deputy Lieutenant]

Gentlemen

I give you noe more trouble at the present then the Sending of a Transcript of the Lords of His Majesties Counsel Letter; for by Experience I am assured of your care and diligence in what concernes his Majesty and his Government so I bid you hartyly farewell.

Lindsey.

Wytham, 19 October 1664

[p. 70]

35. [The Privy Council to the Earl of Lindsey]

After our hearty Commendations to your Lordship

Wheras his Majesties Service at the present doth require a great number of Marriners and Seafaring men to be impressed and imployed for the fitting anf furnishing and compleate maning of his Majesties ffleete of Shipps for which purpose his Royall Highness the Duke of Yorke, Lord High Admirall of England, hath issued severall warrants unto the Vice Admirall of the Marittin Countyes, Citties and Townes and places of this Kingdom for the due execution and effec-

tual performance of this his Majesties soe Important Service. Wee doe hereby pray and require you Lordship immediately to give stricke charge and Command to all the Deputy Lieutenants and allso the justices of the Peace within your Lieutenancy and to all other officers of Corporations within the same to be ayding and assisting unto the said Vice Admiralls and their Deputyes and all such others as are or shall be from time to time appointed and Authorized to imprest Marriners and Seafaring men or the like for Sea Service. And for as much as we find that many Marriners and Seafaring men who have been impresst after that they Received their coat and conduct mony have neglected to appeare according to their Tickets at the places appointed and others after suche appearance have departed from the service without any Lawful discharge and have run into the Inland countryes and absent themselves to the great diservice of his Majesty. His Majesty expects thereuppon and Commands that all his officers and Ministers in authority doe take care that the Lawes in this and the like cases be duly executed uppon such person or persons who shall be proved Delinquents in this kind and we doe heerby pray and require of your Lordship and your Deputyes and all Justices of the Peace to be ayding and assisting to all persons as shall be imployd to find out and prosecute all such offenders and cause them to be apprehended and imprisoned and that notice of all such be given to the board and that further Order may be taken in their Exemplary punishment according to Law and not douting of your Lordships more then ordinary Care in this business of So important consequence we bid your Lordship very heartyly farewell
from the Court at Whitehall this 14 day October 1664
Your Lordships loving freinds
Clarendon, Gilbert Cantuar, Ormond, St Albondes, Angelsey, Lawderdale, Humphry London. George Carteret, John Barkly. William Morris, Henry Bennet
I received this letter this 28 October and sent it to Sir H Heron the very same houer

[pp. 70–71]

36. [The King to the Earl of Lindsey]

To our Right Trusty and Right well beloved Couzine and Councellor Montague Earle of Lindsey Great Chamberlaine of England and Lord Lieutenant of the County of Lincoln[1]

Right Trusty and Right Well beloved Counsellor Wee Greet you well: Whereas in the Act for ordering the forces in the Severall Countyes, it is provided that in case of apparant danger to the Government; It shall and may be lawfull for us to cause to be levied such summe or summes of money dureing the space of 3 yeares from the 25 June 1662 not exceeding the summe of £70,000 for one whole year for the defraying the whole or suche part of the Militia as we shall find our selfe Obliged to imploy in order to the Security and quiet of this Nation: Pursuant to which we did by the advice of our Privy Counsel the last two years respectively send Letters[2] to our respective Lieutenants and their Deputyes to cause the aforesaid summ or summes to be paid in the severall Counties, being thereunto moved by the apparant danger in which the Government was by the plotts and conspircyes of sume unquiet Spirits who had designed the Subversion therof. And wheras there remaines still in the hand of the Sherriff or Sherriffs or of the Collectors or receviers of our said County Severall summes of mony Collected for the two last yeares by vertue of the said Act of Parliament, Our will and pleasure is, that you, your Deputies or some three or more of them Doe forthwith call the said Sheriff or Sheriffs, the Collectors and Receivers of our said County for the two last yeares to exact accompt of how much of the said monyes have been by them respectively Collected and Received, how much issued out, and disposed of, and what therof is now remaining in their or any of their hands; And their Accompts haveing strictly examined them or so much thereof as you, your Deputies or some three or more of them shall think fit, or just to allow, and such part of the said monys as shall after their accompt soe allowed be found remaineing in their or any of their hands be forthwith Recevied by you or your Deputyes or some 3 or more of them.

And they the said Sherriff or Sherriffs, Collectors and Receivers and every of them are hereby required to make speedy payment thereof accordingly which monies or the remainder thereof so received shall by you, your Deputies or some 3 or more of them be fairely told and put into a Trunke or Chest to which there shall be 3 Lockes and Keyes (the charge wherof shall be allowed out of the said monies) one of which Keyes shall remaine in your hands and the other 2 in the hands of your said Deputy Lieutenants chosen by the rest, and the said Trunke or Chest shall be by you or their Order delivered unto the Governor of the Castle or Garrison next adjacent to your Lieutenancy if any such shall be within ten miles of the same. And in case we have no Castle or Garrison within that distance then into suche Towne or place within your Lieutenancy as you or your Deputy Lieutennants or any 3 or more of them shall think most expedient for the safety thereof to be there kept, for which our said Govenor or in his absence our Deputy Govenor shall give his acknowledgment to the end that the said monies may remaine in safe custody untill we shall signifie or further order for the disbursment thereof which shall be to the end appointed by the said Act, and not otherwise. Likewise our Will and pleasure is that you forthwith Certifie us what and how any part of the aforesaid summes for the two last years respectively have been disbursed and if any omission or defect have happened in the passeing or issuing forth thereof that you cause a Stricke inquiry to be made there upon. In which the said high Sherriff or High Sherriffs together with the respective Collectors and Receivers are to be answerable. And further it is our Will and pleasure that our Officers and Souldiers doe 14 dayes duty this next year as they did for the last yeare and for the encouragement of the Officers who shall do duty for the 14 dayes this next year your selfe and the 2 Deputy Lieutenants aforesaid (out of the monyes that shall be paid as aforesaid) are to pay to such person or persons As you our Lieutenant and the said 2 Deputyes or any other 3 Deputy Lieutenants or more of them shall appoint what monies shall be necessarye for the payment of 14 dayes pay in the year to the Comission Officers of Horse and ffoot within your Lieutenancy from a Captain inclusive downwards if so much duty be by them done within your the time aforesaid according to the following Establishment; Viz, To a Captain of Horse per diem 10/-, To a Lieutenant of Horse six shillings, to a Cornet ffive shillings and to a quarter Master of Horse four shillings per diem, To a Captain of ffoot per diem 8/-, To a Lieutenant four shillings and to an ensigne 3 shillings per diem. And the Receite of the person or persons to whome you and the said two Deputy Lieutenants shall pay those monies by the order aforesaid shall be unto you and them as a good ample and sufficient discharge for soe much as you and they shall pay. And you are likewise to take care that the Serjants Corporalls and Drummers be paid out of the Weekes pay ordered by the Act for the providing Trophyes and paying non comissioned Officers 2/- and 6 pence per diem to a Serjeant, and 2/- a day to a Corporall and Drummers for 14 dayes duty in the yeare[3] and in case the said Weekes pay shall fall shorte the said Non Comissiond officers are to be paid out of the monyes that shall be raysed uppon defaultors. And because we have been given to understand that some of the said Lord Lieutenants and Deputy Lieutenants of the respective Countyes have neglected to put their forces upon Duty according to the Act We have thought fit hereby effectually to recommend it to you and your Deputyes forthwith to give order that the fforces within your Lieuteanncy do enter uppon duty and continue constantly from time to time to doe it according to the said Act for which these our Letters shall be unto you and your Deputyies as like wise to the Hygh Sherriff and high Sherriffs of that our County, the Collectors and Receivers and all others respectively a sufficient Warrant and discharge. Given at our Court at Whytehall the 31 day of December in the 16th yeare of our reign

By his Majesties Command

William Morice

[pp. 76–78]
[1] This address is at the foot of the transcript.
[2] Cf. OB 2, 22.
[3] Cf. OB 16.

37. [The Earl of Lindsey to the Deputy Lieutenants]

To the Right Honourable George Viscount Castleton, Lord Willughby[1] of Earsby and the rest of the Deputy Lieutenants of the County of Lincolne.

I have herewith sent you a Transcript of his Majesties Letter of Directions to me given at Whytehall the 31 of December last, and take this opportunity of meeting of the Assizes at Lincolne to committ to your care and dilligence the putting the same in execution wherin amongst other things I conceive you will think fitt to observe these particulars following

1st To give order for all the Milita forces both horse and foot within my Lieutenancy to be in readyness to perform their 14 dayes duty as his Majesties service and the Security of the County shall require.

2nd To call the ffoot upon 7 dayes duty to be performed by the severall Companies to begin at the respective Places hereafter mentioned on the ffifth day of April next unles at Lincolne where the duty is to begin on 4th day of May.

3 Sir Henry Bellassis owne Company to come upon the Guards at Lincolne as allso Lieutenat Colonel Neviles Captain Ryly and Sir Thomas Meeres companyes by halfe a Company at a time or in lesse numbers as you shall think fitt.

4 The residue of Sir Henry Belasis Regiment to come uppon Guards a Company at a time; halfe therrof at Louth and the other halfe at Grimsby or Wainffleet and Captain Pickerings Company in the Regiment of Sir Henry Heron to performe its duty halfe a Company at a time at Wainffleet which

will give an advantage of 2 weekes for part of Sir Henry Belassis Regiment to be at Grimsby more then they are at Wainffleet.

5   The Residue of Sir Henry Herons Company to come uppon the Guards halfe a Company at Boston and other halfe at Spalding or Sutton.

6   The Residue of Sir John Newtons Regiment to come uppon Guard at the places aforesaid in the parts of Holland if they be not necessarily imployed else where.

7   To Reserve the duty of the Horse as long as you can soe as they performe the same some time before the 24 of July next, unless you find it necessary to call them uppon duty sooner as any emergency shall require. All which I leave to your prudence and good Inspection to alter at pleasure as occation may happen for his Majesties service and the safety of the Country. I desire you will take the Accompt of the late Sheriffs for the two Monthes Tax and after you have given allowances according to the Act and his Majesties Former Instructions that you will deduct what is to be paid to the Commission Officers for this years service (which I conceive best to be put into hands of Mr John Thornton Treasure for the Weekes Assessment of whom I desire you to take Security for the payment of it out according to Order) And to certifie me the remaining summe due uppon the said accompts. I doubt not but from time to time you will accquaint me with your proceedings herein that his Majestie may be informed of the due execution of his Commands hereby transmitted to you

Your affectionate Friend
Lindsey

Sir John Buck will pay in the monies at Lincolne upon the 16 of May next. In the meantime I suppose you will get a Chest. I conceive Sir John Munson and Sir Thomas Hussey ffitt persons to be chosen to keep two of the Keyes and I have desired Sir Thomas Meres to keep the 3d key for me

[pp. 79–80]
[1] Lord Willoughby has been omitted from the heading.

38. To the Executors of Sir Edward Dymock lately deceased, To John Thornton gent and late Under sherriff to Sir Edward Dymock lately deceased and late high sherriff of the County of Lincolne, To Sir John Buck knt and Bart late High Sherriff of the County of Lincolne.

Whereas wee[1] have Received Directions from his Majestie, transmitted unto us by the Right Honourable the Earle of Lindsey Lord Great Chamberlaine, Thereby impowering us or any three or more of us to call you and every one of you to an exact accompt of what summe or summes of mony you have respectively Collected and Received for the 2 monthes and 2 Weekes Assessment upon the County for the 2 yeares last past and how much thereof hath been by you issued out and disposed of and which part thereof is still remaining in your hands, These are therefor to require you And every of you to give your parsonall attendance before us or any 3 or more of us upon Tuesday the 21th instant at the signe of The Angell in Lincolne by 9 of the Clocke in the morning then and there to give an exact accompt of what you have done in the premises that we may signifie the same unto his Majestie and to our Lord Lieutenant; hereof faile not at your perill. Given under our hand and seales at Lincolne this 10 of March in the 17 yeare and 1665

[pp. 80–81]
1 'by the Act of the present Parliament passed on the 9th day of February last past' has been crossed out.

39. [The Deputy Lieutenants to the Earl of Lindsey][1]

To my Lord of Lindsey from Lincolne the 10 of March 1665

My Lord, Having received a Transcript of his Majesties Letter to you dated the 31 of December last Inclosed in one from your Lordship of the 4 of March instant with directions for bringing of our forces upon 7 dayes duty by halfe a Company at a time, wee humbly presume to represent to your Lordship the present condition of our Country which is allmost desperate there being very little seed gott into the ground this Spring and that probable lost by reason of the extremity of the violent frost and snow which at present doth lye very deep uppon the ground, and therfore humbly begg that the duty of the foot which will take away many of the husbandmen persons and Servants may be respited till the middle of May that the farmers may be the better both to mantayne himselfe and ffamily and pay the dutyes granted to his Majesty; and if your Lordship conceive it necessary that the Militia performe their dutyes this yeare this delay may be supplyed by calling whole Companies together and more at a time which we conceive will be no wayes disadvantagous to the Discipline of the Militia nor of danger to the Country haveing not any apprehension of the least Insurrection in these parts which is all the trouble your Lordship shall at present receive from
Your

We humbly desire to receive speedily your Lordships hearing and shall observe your commands concerning the accompts.

[p. 81]
1 The senders of the letter are not listed.

40. [Proceedings in the Privy Council 31 March 1665]

At the Court of Whitehall last of March 1665

The Kings Most Excellent Majestie Present
Lord Archbishop of Canterbury, Lord Chancellor, Lord Treasurer, Duke of Albermarle, Duke of Ormond, Marquis of Dorchester, Lord Great Chamberlaine, Lord Chamberlaine, Earl of Berkshire, Earl of Angelsey, Earl Lauderdale, Earl Carberry, Lord Bishop of London, Lord Arlington, Lord Berkley, Lord Ashley, Mr Treasurer, Mr Vice Chamberlaine, Mr Chancellor of the Duchy, Sir Edward Nicholas.

Whereas it was this day represented to his Majestie in Counsell by the Right Honourable Earle of Lindsey Lord Great Chamberlain of England and his Majesties Lieutenant for the County of Lincolne that the Constables of Market Deeping in the County of Lincolne having assessed that town for the payment of the men sent by order of the Deputy Lieutenants according to the supplementall Act for the Militia[1] to doe duty in Major Conyers Company and rated one Bird a Chandler at 2s 6d which he refusing to pay the said Constables obteyned a Warrant from the Deputy Lieutenants to distraine for the said money which haveing putt in execution the said Bird by the Instigation of one Mapletoft an Attorney sued the Constables for the same in the 3 weekes court at Deeping and that by the combination of the said Atturney and the Deputy Steward of the Court the Constables where cast, whereby his Majesties Officers are much discouraged from endeavering the puting of the Act for the Militia in Execution. It was therefore ordered by His Majesty in Counsell that Sir William Trollope or some other of his Majesties Deputy Lieutenants shall be prayed and required and they are hereby prayed and required to send for the said Bird the Chandler, Mapletoft the Atturny and Mr Hill the Deputy Steward and to take bonds of them to appeare before the Lords of His Majesties Privy Counsell in our Consell Chamber at Whytehall on the 14th day of April next and therfore not to faile as they will answer the contrayes at their perill[2]

John Nicholas

[pp. 83–84]
[1] 15 Charles c.4.
[2] Cf. OB 44.

41. [The Earl of Lindsey to the Deputy Lieutenants]

By my former Letters dated from hence the 4 of March the last past I signified to you (Amongst other things) his Majesties pleasure that the remaininge summe of the Monthes Tax for 2 yeares should be placed in a Chest, which Sir John Buck will pay in at Lincolne on the 16 day of May next, at which time I desire you to meet there concerning the same and to consult and put in execution the Acts and his Majesties Instructions for ordering the Militia; I doe conceive you will thinke it convenient to have the generall meetings more frequently and so from this to adjoyrne from time to time as may seeme best to you for his Majesties service which doubtless will be the better promoted by your debates and consultations at those meetings, the want thereof as been the occation I conceive of the Exception made by Sir John Munson to the order at Louth 26 of August 1664.[1] A Coppie whereof being presented to me I acquaint you with it and doe hould it convenient to alter the Lists formerly returned to me, but uppon good Consideration by the consent of the Major part of you at a Generall meeting; therefore I would have those Horse lately ordered to serve in Captain Bolls Troop which are belonging unto Sir John Munsons Troop to continue as they served before under Sir John Munson and doe desire (as I did formerly in a Letter dated from Grimsthorpe the 26th of September last to the Deputy Lieutennents acting in Louth and Hornecastle Sessions) that you will have so diligent an inspection into the values of the Estates returned or you shall be informed of, that his Majesties forces be not lessened which was formerly given me in the Lysts and this I insisted uppon then as allsoe now by reason of Captain Bolls complaint to me that he wanted 13 Horse when he was uppon duty at Lincolne that where assigned him in his Lyst but how the same is falne so short I have not had as yet any accompt, therefore desire your Circumspection and good agreement in all things touching his Majesties sevice which will be most acceptable to your affectionate friend

Lindsey

Westminster, 6 April 1665.

[p. 82]
¹ Cf. OB 42.

42. [Order of the Deputies meeting at Louth]

Louth August 26 1664
It is then ordered that the persons underwritten being within the Sessions of
Caster doe appear and serve according to their proportion compleately armed in
the Troop of Captain John Boll

Brocklesby	Charles Pellam Esq	1 Horse
Barton ⎫ Ulceby ⎭	Mr Edward Melthorpe ⎫ Mr Thomas Apleyard ⎭	1 Horse
Thornton Colledge ⎫ Barton ⎭	Mr Skinner ⎫ Mr John Sands ⎭	1 Horse
Thornton	Sir George Wynne one ⎫ And the other ⎭	2 Horse
Gophill	Henry Hillyard Esq	
Caster	Mr Alex Emerson Mr Farrar	1 Horse

Willoughby
William Wray
Adrian Scroope
Martin Lister

[p. 83]

43. To the Right Honourable the Earl of Lindsey

May it please your Lordship
At a meeting at Corby we appointed the Guards of the Holland forces Horse and
ffoott to be sett thus

Colonel Sir Henry Herons to begin duty at Spalding	on the 4th of May
Lieutenant Colonel Thomas Thory at Boston	on the 18 of May
Major Edmond Ogars at Spalding	the 15 of June
Captain William Spooner at Long Sutton	the 1st of June
Captain William Oldfeild at Spalding	the 29 of June
Captain Lawrence Pickering at Wainfleet	the 6th of July
the time left to the Deputy Lieutenants in Lindsey coast	
Captain Booths Company at Boston	the 1st of June
Sir Anthony Oldfeilds Troop at Spalding	the 7th of July

If your Lordship please to have any of these altered we humbly intreate wee may
receive your Commands and upon the Recepit of your Lordships order we will
send out orders to the Major or in his absence to the next Captain in the Country
which are but two Captain William Oldfeild and Captain Pickering; we doe likewise humbly desire to know your Lordships pleasure that if we heare the Navies
are engaged whether some of them shall not be sooner set uppon duty the better

to secure the Coastside and that every Company but Captain Pickerings may march once in their 14 dayes to Boston, Spalding and Sutton they having allready learnt their Discipline but doe not as yet well know how to march; we waite to receive and obey your Lordships furder Commands as becometh

Your Lordships most humble and obedient
Servants
William Trollope, Robert Markham, Anthony Oldfeild

from Corby the 13 of April 1665

[p. 85]

44. [Mr Edward Christian to Sir Anthony Oldfield][1]

Sir Anthony

I formerly acquainted you with an order for Hill, Bird and Mapletoft to attend the Counsell Board[2] as yesterday where they accordingly did to make their defence touching the suit commenced against the Constable of Deeping for taking a distress by the Deputy Lieutenants Warrant, his Majestie was present in the Counsell. Hills crime was not soe greate as the other two Soe by his submission and begging his Majesties pardon was dismissed with a Checke, the other two Bird and Mapletoft the Atturny are Committed to the ffleet; there was present Deputy Lieutenants the two Sir Thomas Munsons, Sir Thomas Meres and Sir Robert Carr. I hope this good example will make the Constables dilligent in those things they are required by the Deputy Lieutenants for his Majesties service when such care is taken for their incouragment; this is all at present from

Edward Christian

[pp. 84–85]
[1] There is no date or heading in the manuscript. PRO PC 2/58, fos 89r, 102r, shows the meeting of the Board was 14 April.
[2] OB 40.

45. [The Earl of Lindsey to the Deputy Lieutenants][1]

I received yours of the 10 the instant whereby I perceive you have agreed an Establishment for the Inferior Officers under the degree of Commission Officers and for other Emergencies to be allowed to the respective Companies and Troopes out of the Weekes Assessment Appointed by the Act of Parliament for defraying the sumes, viz for a Captain of ffoot £15 per annum and for a Captain of a Troop of Horse £18 per annum. I am glad for the encouragement. It will hould out so muche concerning the Trophies already provided; I conceive it the same thing as if they were yet to provide, since that the weekes Assessment will not afford more then what you have set downe for the respective Compamies and Troopes out of what remaines. I must recommend to you what is fit to be allowed to those Clerkes that have taken paines or shall be necessarily employed about setling the Militia and there may happen other occations in order to his Majesties service which may require an expence of mony for which it is good to keep a reserve. I shall remind you of the rayseing the Weekes Assessment for this year when you find it most conveneint to doe it; your proceedings in puting the Act in execution against the persons charged with Armes that make default is very acceptable to me and I desire you will persevere in it that his Majesties service may be effectually performed within my Lieutenancy.

[p. 93]
[1] The letter has neither heading nor date.

46. The names of such as was thought fitt to give in Bonds to his Majestie.

Spittle Sessions
Captain Spilman of Walkwood
Captain Munckton
Robert Ruckill
John Kelsey and
Johnathon Grant

Grantham
Maurice Dalton[1]
Mr William Clarke
Mr Brynes
Mr Walls
Mr Garnor but not bound.
Cornet Boole
Mr Richard
Mr Rocket
Renolds
Honman
Cornet Tigh
Lacy

Castor Session
Pim
Urry
Edward Nelthorp
Bartholmew Ornes

Horncastle Sessions
Robert Preston
Butler

Holland
The Late Major Tylday[2]

Bourne Sessions
Noel Butler
John Cole

Sleaford
Peter Bunworth
King Edward at Lincoln[3]
Bruntall
William Tompson

(These Prisoned down at Lincoln)

These following persons bound at Sleaford, Boston and Spalding (except Thomas Joanes of Horncastle) by Sir Anthony Oldfeild and Sir Robert Carr

Thomas Joanes of Horncastle
John Right
Richard Northam of Harlexton
Mr Drake
Mr Thomas Birnwork
William Morris

At Spalding
Nathaniel Gregory and John Neale of St Edmonds
Mr John Craycrafte ⎫
Thomas Kirke   ⎪
Thomas Dawson   ⎬ Committed to Lincoln[4]
James Garner   ⎭
Goodales of Moulton
William Simons of Gedney
Mr Barrington a stranger
Richard Owen   Not bound

At Boston
John Whaly on   50
William Cooper   50
Mr Ben Wythering   200
Mr Robert Yarborough   100
Mr Benjamin Ludlam   50
Mr John Tooly   200[5]
Thomas Sanderson   100
Mr Thomas Welby   200[6]
Mr Thomas Tooly   200
Mr Ralph Harrison   500
Gooses   05

The Condition

The Condition of this Obligation is such that if the above bounden A. B. do personally appear at the Angell in the Bayle of Lincoln uppon the sixth of March before the Deputy Lieutenants of the County of Lincoln and that in the meane time he be of good peaceable demeanor towards the Soveraign Lord the King and all his liege people and that he appeare at such convenient place as he shall be directed by a writting signed by the Lord Lieutenant of this County or two of his Deputy Lieutenants at the place of his abode and within 24 hours after such writing is soe left unless he leave to be absent uppon his just occacions granted under the hand and seale of 2 or more of the Deputy and that he discover all plots and conspiracies against His Majesty or his Government that he shall know off. And abstaine and keeep from Conventicles and all other seditious meetings. Given etc

The warrant to bring them in

In prosecution of His Majesties special command for the presevation of the Peace of this County. These are to apprehend   [7] And to bring   [7] Before us at the   [7] In   [7] or before the 10 September. Given etc.

[pp. 99–100]
[1] For Dalton, see Bill Couth (transcr.), *Grantham during the Interregnum: The Hall Book of Grantham 1641–1649* (LRS lxxxiii, 1995), 88, 136.
[2] Possibly Mayor Tilson of Boston. See J. F. Bailey, *Transcription of minutes of the Corporation of Boston* (4 vols, Boston, 1980–85), iii. 276.
[3] For Colonel Edward King, see Introduction, p. xxvi.
[4] Kirke is not amongst those listed as imprisoned at Lincoln: PRO, SP 29 134/13.
[5] Tooly was a former mayor of Boston (*Minutes of the Corporation of Boston*, iii. 295).
[6] For Welby, see OB 85, article 10.
[7] Blanks in the manuscript.

47. [Orders from a meeting of the Deputy Lieutenants][1]

August the 30th 1665[2]

Order that the powder in the Magazine be sould out to the Souldiers at a lower rate then the shop keepers upon the next duty.

2 That every Captain of Horse may have 20lb of powder out of the Magazine upon account and 60lb of bullet uppon emergency. And that every Captain of ffoot may have 90lb of powder and 15lb of bullet upon the like emergency and the match to be proportioned or conjoined amongst the Companyes

3 That the Deputy Lieutenants meet hear againe uppon Tuesday come three weekes.

4 That in pursuance of a former order Mr Thornton Treasurer doe give an account at the next meeting of the Deputy Lieutenants of which moneys he hath Received and disbursed of the Weekes Tax since his last account and that a Coppy of this order be sent to him.

[p. 99]
[1] The letter does not have a heading.
[2] The line before the date has been left blank.

48. [The King to the Earl of Lindsey]

To Our Right Trusty and Right well beloved Couzin and Counsellor Mountague Earl of Lindsey our Great Chamberlayne of England Lord Lieutenant of the County of Lincolne or in his absence to our trusty and well beloved The Deputy Lieutenants and to be delivered to the Deputy Lieutenant nearest the ffirst Stage in the County of Lincolne by him to be forthwith communicated to the rest of them.

Hast Extraordinary Post hast for his Majesties most Speciall Service.

Charles Rex

Right Trusty and Right well beloved Couzin and Counsellor and trusty and well beloved, We greet you well. Having lately received severall Intelligences from abroad which give us great cause to apprehend that there is an Invasion intended upon this our kingdom by foraigne Enemies; We thought fitt to signfie our pleasure unto you hereby requireing and expresely commanding that you forthwith draw together into a body all the militia of that our County of Lincolne both Horse and ffoot whome you are to put in a Good posture and place them uppon their Guard at or neare such Port or Ports or upon such coasts of the Sea as you shall judge most convenient to discover and opose the Landing of any forces. And we do further require that you take speciall Care and give Speedy Order to have the Beacons of our said County well repaired and constantly watched by sufficient persons and to be fired where there shall be occasion; that you doe performe all other things necessary or tending to the common safety in Juncture according to the Trust we repose in you and that Vigilance and dilligence which we promise our selfe from you and soe bid you farewell. Given att our Court at Oxford 25 January In the 17 Yeare of our Reign.

By his Majesties Command
William Morrice

Oxford	3 in the afternoon Fryday
Brackly	9 at night
Tosset	2 in the morning
Norton	8 of the Clock 27 of January
Geddington	12 of the Clock
Stamford	3 of the Clock
Spalding	at 2 of the Clock Afternoon

[p. 94]

49. [Orders of the Deputy Lieutenants]

Orders at Lincolne the 2 of February 1666

Ordered that the whole Militia both horse and ffoot in Lindsie have their head Quarters at Louth:
Order; And that the whole Milita both Horse and ffoot in Kesteven and Holland shall have their head Quarters at Boston:
Order; That the said Militia of Kesteven and Holland do keep Guard at Wainfleet and from thence South ward.
And that the Militia in Lindsey Coast do guard all the other coasts belonging to the County of Lincoln.
That horse be placed at Boston, Spalding, Sutton or Holbech.
That the Lord Willoughbyes Troop be at Boston if his Lordship do not make choyce of one of the other two places changing with one of the other Captains.
That Sir Anthony Oldfeilds Troop be at Spalding.
That Captain Thorolds Troop be at Sutton or Holbech.
That Sir John Munsons Troop be placed at Louth.
That Captain Thyrwiths Troop be placed at Saltfleet or Alford
That Captain Bolles Troop be at Grimsby.
Lindsey Foot
    That the Deputy Lieutenants or any two or more of them meeting at Louth do Order the distribution of the foot in Sir Henry Bellewes Regiment to such outguards as they shall find best from time to time.
Kesteven and Holland Foot
    That the Deputy Lieutenants or any two or more of them, meeting at Boston doe Order the distribution of the foot in Kesteven and Holland regiments to such out guards as they shall find best from time to time.
Order that a Souldier of every Troop be always at the respective head Quartors for conveying orders.

That all the Militia both of Horse and ffoot do meet at their respective head Quarters on Thursday the 8 of February instant.

That no person serving as a Volunteer Souldier shall be freed from any charge towards the Militia whereunto he is liable by the Militia Act.

The Warrant then agreed upon.

These are in pursuance of his Majesties express commands will and require you upon Sight hereof to issue out your Warrant to all the Petty Constables within your division requiring them and every of them that they Summon and warn every foot souldier within their Severall Parishes and Constabularyes belonging to the Regiment of [1] To appear at [1] Uppon the   day of [1] next, provided with pay powder and bullets and other necessaries for 14 dayes duty. Every Musquetteer is to bring with him 4 pounds of powder and 4lbs of bullet and if he serve with a matchlock Tenn yards of match all which are to [be] provided at the charge of the Armes ffinders and you or your Petty Constables are likewise to require all the persons charged to find Armes within you Libertie or jurisdiction: to make good their Severall charges wherof you and your Petty Constables are to take good care and provide that the said severall charges be duely answered where two or more are charged to find one ffoot Armes, and you and they shall [be] reimburst what shall be expended thereupon by an Assessment; with power of distres and Sale in case of non-payment uppon demand. You and your Petty Constables are likewise to warne all persons in your respective Libertie and charged towards horse to cause their severall charges to appeare at the time and place aforesaid compleately Horst Armed and furnished with pay, powder and bullets for 14 dayes; hereof you and your Petty Constables are not to faile.

And you the chief Constables are to take care with all possible speed to erect and prepare for the present use every Beacon formerly used within your Division to provide all materialls fit for the use and firing of the same and that every of them be constantly watched until further order and set on fire immediately upon the ffireing of any other Beacon within view and all this to be done at the charge of Such as the law requires; you are therefore to layout the mony for doeing the same and you shall be reimburst.

Henry Bellowes, John Monson, Robert Markham, Anthony Oldfeild, John Newton, John Monson, Edward Rossiter, William Trollope, Robert Carr, Thomas Meres, William Wray.

[pp. 97–98]
[1] Blanks in the manuscript.

50. [Orders of the Deputy Lieutenants]

Orders[1] Agreed upon at Boston the 8th of February 1666 By the Deputy Lieutenants for the better circumspect watch and regard to be given to the ffire beacons within the County of Lincolne.

It is ordered that the said Beacons shall be presently repaired and fully furnished sufficiently provided with flax and pitch as hath been accustomned and that the flax and pitch be presently delivered to the Custodie and Keeping of Surveyors there to remaine ready at all times to be putt in use as cause shall require and not to be delivered to any man without the consent of one or more of the persons hereafter named and appointed Surveyors of the said Beacons.

It is ordered that the said Beacons be orderely watched and warily kept by the Inhabitants of the Townes accustomned both by day and night viz. Two by the day and three by the night; and that speciall care be all wayes had by the Constables of every Towne that one at the least appointed to watch day and night be an househoulder of honest behaviour and discretion.

It is ordered that the said Watchmen shall continue from time to time to take their charge of watch of one of the Constables of the Towne where they inhabite and that the said Constables shall in his Majesties name charge and command them that they and every of them continue the Watch by day from Sunrise till Sun Set and for night from the seting of the Sun till the Riseing of the same, and like-wise shall have speciall regard unto the Beacons on the Sea Coasts and that if they see any Beacons fired and that one of them with all speed give knowledge therof to one of the said surveyors or to any Justice of the Peace or to any Commission Officer.

If they shall see any Ships above the number of Six suspitiouslly to ride to and fro on the Sea coast over against their coast that then they forthwith one of them give knowledg therof to one of the said Surveyors or any justice of the peace or Comission officer, or if they shall see or perceive any person or persons to attempt the ffiring of the said Beacons without the assent of one of the surveyors or put in practice any unlawful act about the same that then they shall not onely to the utmost of their powers stay all Suche persons but allso endeavor themselves to take the same and give speedy intelligence thereof to one of the said Surveyors or to any justice of the Peace or Commissioned Officers.

If the watchmen shall See any number of ships or one ship landing any number of men suspitiously that one of them with all speed give knowledge thereof to one of the said Surveyors or to any justice of the peace or Commis-sioned Officers.

Orders for the Surveyors

It is ordered that A.H and J. S. Shall be surveyors of the Beacon in the Wapentake of S.[1] and that they and any of them shall have a speciall care to see these orders duely kept.

It is ordered that if any watchman shall give to any of them Intelligence of the ffiring of any Beacon or of the suspitious Landing of any number of men or of the lying or rideing of any ships above the number of six or of any attempting to ffire or do any unlawful act about the said Beacon that then he and they to whom such intelligences shall be given calling for further assistance therein shall forthwith with all possible speed give knowledg thereof to the next Justice of the Peace and presently repaire to the said Beacon and put all things in readines for the ffireing thereof untill further advise be had herein from the Justices of the Peace, except that apparant shew of eminent danger by Suspitious Landing of men do informe the more speedy fireing of the said Beacons.

It is ordered that the said Surveyors shall from time to time repaire to the said Beacons and have due regard that the said watch be duely kept by sufficient persons for the charge and if they find any default to Certifie the same forthwith to one of the Constables of the Town whose charge is to watch, who shall pres-ently bring the person remissive or makeing default before some Justice of the Peace to answere his Misdeamenor in that behalfe.

Orders to be observed by the Justices of the Peace

That upon notice given to any of them or any just Cause ministred for the fireing of any Beacon that forthwith they or some of them give knowledg therof to the Lord Lieutenant or some of his Deputy Lieutenants and if apparrant danger shall seem to fall out to the Country before the return of any answer and direction from the Lord Lieutenant or his Deputy that then presently the Justices shall warne or cause to be warned all the persons as well appointed to Armes, as alsoe of abillity to watch, and any force presently to repaire to such convenient place as shall be appointed and thought most fitt for the with standing the enemies force and that they so warned and assembled together have Sufficient Victualling for the space of two or three days at the least.

If any danger appear by Suddaine Invasion to the hazard of lives loss of goods, ffiring of buildings or any other spoile or depopulation of the Country that then they cause the people not serviceable of defence speedily to remove and convey themselves and all manner of goods and chattels moveable and supportable into the higher parts of the Country for their better safety and surer refuge.

For the nameing of the Surveyors of the Beacons more speedily we do require the chiefe Constables to name or appoint the most able and sufficient men next adjoyning and to return their name to us with what convenient speed they may; that we may alter or allow of them as occasion shall serve.

[pp. 95–96]
[1] Skirbeck.

51. [The King to the Earl of Lindsey]

Charles Rex

Right Trusty and Right well beloved Couzen We greet you well[1]
Whereas uppon severall intelligences from abroad we have reason to doubt that there are preparations made by our Enemies towards an Invasion of this our Kingdome we have thought fitt to secure ourselves and Subjects in the best manner we can from their attempts, and in order thereunto have concluded it requisite to put the Militia of the Kingdome in a good posture of defence, ffor which purpose we doe thereby require and expressely command you forthwith to repayre to some convenient place within your Lieutenancy to unite the Gentry and quicken all under your command to the discharge of their respective duties and put into execution those and what other Instructions you shall from time to time receive from us, that soe the milita within your precincts be in a readynes if there shall be an occasion to make use of them. You are therefore in the first place to take care that all your Companyes of ffoot and Troopes of Horse be compleate according to your late Established Settlement and if any of them are dead since the last Muster or are removed out of your Lieutenancy that their places be filled with able and sufficient men makeing up likewise the number of your Officers compleate, taking further care to order that their Armes be all fixed and they have in readynes a sufficient quantity of Ammunicion of powder match and bullet as the Act of Parliament concerning the Militia directs, and for avoiding more expense and trouble to the Country then is needful in this time of Harvest this may be done for the present (unless more danger arrive) without either generall or particular Musters by sending for and giving order to all your ffield officers and Captains that they make diligent inquiry after those particulars and when

they have rightly Informed themselves thereof they accordingly accquaint you with it upon which you are forthwith to give an account to the Lords of our Counsell not only of each Troop and Company but also in what condition and readiness they now are. And for the making a more speedy and quick resistance in case of Invasion, You may appoint certain Posts or places of Rendezvous within your Lieutenancy where your Souldiers may resort and make head uppon all Alarmms, where the Deputy Lieutents next adjacent are to be present assigning them their particular Quartors and Precincts . . .[1]

[p. 113]

[1] The transcript ends at this point. From BL Add MS 39,246, fo 16v, we can complete the letter:

within which they shall command in such Cases And for the preventions of any surprise in this nature, you are to take espetiall Care and give speedy order that the Beacons be watched by sufficient persons within the respective hundreds neare adjoining the Seaside and fired as there shall be occasion. And wheras the Act of Parliament ordeynes a weekes Assessment after the Rate of £70000 per month shall be raysed and levyed yearly for the defraying of necessary Charges, and makeing some allowances to the Inferior Officers, you are immediately to rayse and by the said summes within your Lieutenancy (if it be not already done).

And we further recommend to you the putting in execution all other Powers with which you are instructed that may lend to the preservation of the publique safety in this Conjuncture according to that care and Dilligence which we promise ourselves from you. And of the whole and what may relate therunto from tyme to tyme to return a full Accompt to the Lords of our Privy Counsell to the End such further order may be given therin as shall be found necessary. And so we bid you farewell. Given at our Court at Whitehall the 25 day of June 1666.

By his Majesties Command
Arlington

52. [The Earl of Lindsey to the Deputy Lieutenants]

To   [1]

Whereas by Instruction from his Majesty we are informed of a probabillity of an Invasion upon this Kingdome, yet his Majesty to avoid expense and trouble as much as is possible in this time of harvest hath onely Commanded the Militia to be ready upon an hours warning for service. These are therefore to Command you to issue out your Warrants to your Petty Constables requiring them to warn all Armes finders in their liberties to provide their souldiers with sufficient Armes well fixed and with pay, powder and match and bullet for 14 dayes duty. And where their Souldiers are dead or removed out of the Lieutenancy that they carry in able and sufficient men to their respective Captain or Chief Officer to be allowed or Listed in their Stead and the said Petty Constables are alsoe to require all Soldiers (both Horse and ffoot) uppon fireing of Beacons or other Sumone immediately to repaire to their Colors; the Horse at Spalding and the ffoot at Boston at the uttmost perills to both Armes finders and Souldiers and you are further Commanded immediately to see that the Beacons in your Liberties be strictly watched and for the better execution thereof you are to provide and hyre Six able and honest men to watch each Beacon, one watching in the Day time and two in the night by turnes and they are to keep fire constantly in the Beacon house and to goe up to the top of them once an hour, and upon the discover of the fireing of any Beacon the watch men is with all speed to repayre to the next Deputy Lieutenant or Justice of the Peace for Direction therein. Given this 11 July 1666.

[p. 116]
¹ Apart from 'To' there is no heading to the letter.

53. The King to the Earl of Lindsey¹

Charles Rex

Right Trusty and Right Well beloved Cozen we greet you well
Whereas the too houses of Parliament now assembled at Westminster, having Received during the Sessions diverse Information of the Insolent Carriage of the Popish Recusants of late in the severall parts of this our Kingdome, and apprehending least their exorbitancies if not timely prevented should at length breake out into a publique disturbance of our Government, have by their late addresses humbly moved us that for prevention thereof all Popish Recusants, or suche as being suspected soe to be should refuse to take the oath of Supremacy and allegiance, might forth with be Soe disarmed as to remove all apprehensions from our good Subjects of their possibility to disturb the Publique Peace.² Wee having taken the same into our Princely Consideration and accepting very gratiously the zeale and Care of our said houses of Parliament in what concernes the good of our people and the safety and quiet of our Government have thought fitt with the advise of our privy Counsell hereby to signify our will and pleasure to you that forthwith uppon receipt hereof you give effectuall order that all Popish Recusants within your Lieutenancy, or such as being suspected soe to be shall refuse to take the oathes of Supremacy and allegiance being tendered to them, be forthwith soe disarmed as to remove all apprehensions of their possibility to disturb the Publique Peace which we recommend to your Especiall care and vigilence to preserve in all occasions against the Malitious contrivances and designes of those whose Interests it may be to disquiet the same, whereof we shall from time to time an account from you and particularly how armed you have found the said Recusants. And for soe doing this shall be your Warrant. And soe we bid you farwell. Given at our Court at Whythall the 24 day of November 1666 in the 18 year of our reigne.
By his Majesties Command
Arlington
And our further will and pleasure is that you receive into your owne hands the Armes you shall by vertue of this our letter be possessed of or appoint the same to be kept by some of your Deputy Lieutenants giving an account to us whereuppon you shall Receive our further pleasure.
Arlington

[pp. 122–23]
¹ Robert Bertie, third Earl of Lindsey, who succeeded his father as lieutenant in July 1666.
² Cf. J. Miller, *Popery and Politics in England 1660–1688* (London, 1973), 103–4.

54. To Sir John Newton and Sir Robert Markham

Sir,

By the last Post wee Received from my Lord Lieutenant a transcript of his Majesties Letter to him (a Coppie whereof we have enclosed)¹ with an intimation from my Lord Secretary that his Lordship desired the Deputy Lieutenants to put it into execution and considering the advantage of a Generall meeting to agree upon one rule and method to proseed by. We have appointed ffryday next being the 7th of December to meet at 10 of the Clock at the Angel in the Bayle of Lincoln, which is as soon as convenient notice can be given into Lindsey and we must desire you will send into Kestiven and Holland which is all but that we are

Your very humble Servants
John Monson
John Monson

Burton November ult 1666

You would do well to send his Majesties Letter into Holland. I am very ill and unable to stir abroad.

Your servant
Robert Markham[2]

[p. 122]
[1] Cf. OB 53.
[2] The note from Markham is written at the bottom of the letter.

55. To Sir Anthony Oldfeild[1]

Sir.

This letter I received on Thursday night at 6 of the Clock, soe not possible to be at the meeting, a Coppie of His Majesties Letter I have here sent unto you. I have intreated Sir John Monson to be pleased to accquaint me what is agreed on at their Generall Meeting. I rest your most humble servant

William Trollope

[p. 122]
[1] The address to Oldfield is at the foot of the letter.

56. [The Earl of Lindsey to the Deputies acting in Holland]

Gentlemen I being informed that the Officers of the Militia that did their duty at or about Boston are yet without their pay, I doe therefore desire you to take care they be dispatched out of the moneys that is raysed out of the Militia.

I am Your affectionate Friend
Lindsey

Lindsey House, 1st December 1666

[p. 124]

57. [The Deputy Lieutenants[1] to the Earl of Lindsey]

To my Lord of Lindsey, December 7 at the Bayle in Lincoln

My Lord. In obedience to his Majesties Commands and the Directions, We this day mett to put the same in Execution but found ourselves not any way impowered by his Majestie, our Comission, or the Lawes to tender the oath of Supremacy to any person either convicted or suspected of Recusancy, neither is there any we know of that stands as yet convicted, and therfore we most humbly desire that you will aquaint his Majestie with the readeness in all things to observe his Commands and our incapassity to proceed further upon his late Instructions unless we may be by a Commission impowerd to tender the said oath to all persons suspected of Recusancie or receive further Directions which is all but that we are

My Lord
Your most humble servants

[p. 124]

1 This is probably the deputies acting in Holland who in OB 25 reported there were no papists in their part of the shire.

58. [The Earl of Arlington to the Earl of Lindsey]

Whitehall, May 29 1667

My Lord

His Majesty understanding that the Dutch are ready in a few dayes to put to Sea with their ffleet and beleiving they will not faile to appeare before the Coast and to give the alarum to the Country and possibly if they find the occation easie make an attempt to Land, with designe at least to burne spoyle and savage what parts they can of the Country. His Majestie out of his gratious care for the safety and quiet of his Subjects hath commanded me to give your Lordship this notice of it, to signifie his pleasure to you that forthwith uppon receipt hereof your Lordship give order that the Militia of that County be in such a readynes that uppon the shortest warning they may assemble and be in Armes for the defence of the Coast in case of any attempt or appearance of the Enemyes ffleet, takeing care in the meantime that the severall Beaconns upon or near the Coast be duely watched by the Respective Hundreds in which they are, for the preventing any Surprise of Suddaine descent of the Enemie; and his Majestie Commands me particularly to mind your Lordship that in all places where you shall be obliged to make head or appear to the Enemy You make the greatest show in number you can and more especially of Horse even though it be of such as are otherwise wholly unfitt and improper for wares service. Horse being Force will most discourage the Enemy from Landing, for any such attempt. The whole his Majestie commands me to be commend to your Lordships best care and vigilance leaving it in the particular Circumstances to your Lordships owne prudence and discression as you shall see the occation upon the Place, desireing from time to time an accompt of what shall happen and the state of all things relating to his Majesties service within that Lieutenancy; I am

My Lord
Your Lordships most humble servant
Arlington

[p. 127]

59. [The Earl of Lindsey to the Deputy Lieutenants]

To the Deputy Lieutenants, Grimsthorp June 1st 1667

Gentlemen,

Having received a letter from my Lord Arlington, a coppy[1] of which I have with the speed I could sent to you, that you finding the danger the Country may be in by the suddain descent of the Enemie may speedily use your diligence for the geting the Militia in readyness, that upon the least notice they may be in armes for the defence of the Coast, and that you will take care the Beaconns be diligently watched desiring you from time to time to give me an account thereof and of what else may happen that I may informe his Majesty thereof; I am

Your affectionate Friend

Lindsey

I have sent Letters alsoe to the other Divisions for the greater Expeditcion.

[p. 128]
1 OB 58.

60. To Sir Henry Heron, Sir Anthony Oldfeild and the rest of the Deputy Lieutenants for the parts of Holland[1]

Gentlemen,

I question not but you are mindfull in sending out your Warrant for the Collecting of the Weekes Tax Granted by Act of Parliament for Trophies, Ammunition and the like, but in regards I hear nothing of the last Years Collection for the said Weekes Tax I cannot but mind you, that you grant forth your Warrant for the Collecting of this yeares Weekes Tax and to give an account of the last which as yet I have not heard of, I am

Your very affectionate Friend

Lindsey

Lett the Chief Constables of your respective Wapentakes keep the monyes in their hands untill they Receive further order as high collectors in their Wapentakes for the payment thereof to such Treasurers as shall be appointed by me.

[p. 128]
1 This letter is undated.

61. [The Privy Council to the Earl of Lindsey]

After our hearty commendations to your Lordship, whereas the present state of affaires may require the speedy calling together of the Forces in the severall counties in order to the securing the Kingdom from forraign Invasion, the Enemy already appearing with a fleet of Shipps upon the coast, we have thought fitt to give you notice thereof to the end speedy warning may be given for all the Horse and ffoot of the Country to be in a readynes to march at a short notice to such places as your Lordship shall find most convenient, or shall be ordered from hence for oposeing the enemie if he shall make any attempt to Land and for the defence of the Country; and for their encouragement and such as shall supply them for their march His Majestie hath declared his Royall pleasure and required us to signifie unto your Lordship that dureing the said fforces continuing in Service after their Rendezvouzing and marching uppon the occation aforesaid they shall be in his Majesties pay as the rest of his Forces. We are by his Majesties Direction further to acquaint you, that upon serious consideration had uppon the Act Intitled an Act for ordering the fforces in the Severall Counties of this Kingdome,[1] It doth appear that although any of the said fforces have formerly been in actuall service for a Month or more, and were provided with a monthes pay, yet nevertheless they in their persons are to appeare and serve when soever they shall be thereunto Summoned as by the said Act doth appeare under penalty therein mentioned; And for the easing of his Majesties charge we pray and require your punctuall care and diligence in the constant rayseing the monyes

designed for furnisheing Ammunition and other necessaryes and the fines due
from defaulters uppon the said Act and to have the same in readines to answer
Emergencies; and not doubting of your Lordships ready complyance with these
his Majesties commands Wee bid your Lordship very heartyly farewell from the
Court at Whyte Hall, the 11th of June 1667.

Your Lordships very Loving Friends

Manchester, Dorchester, Anglesee, Bathe, Bridgwater, Craven, Lauderdaill,
Fitzharding, Ashly, Arlington, John Berkley, Thomas Clifford, William Morrice,
William Coventry, Richard Browne.

Postscript

Richard Browne

Since the writing hereof finding that your Lordship (amongst some other Lord
Lieutenants of this Kingdome) hath failed to return to the Board a Lyst of the
severall Troopes and Companyes of Militia in the County under your care with
the numbers in them severally as you were required; We do pray and require your
Lordship the next Post after receipt hereof as you will tender the safety of his
Majesties kingdom to send the same unto us and therin also express as many of
the Commission officers names as your Lordship can by that time ascertaine

Richard Browne

[pp. 129–30]
[1] 14 Charles II c.3, s.vi.

62. To Sir Henry Heron, Sir Anthony Oldfeild, and the rest of the Deputy Lieutenants in the parts of Holland.

Gentlemen,

Having just now Received a Letter from the Counsell a Coppy of which I have
inclosed and thereby finding that this County may be in danger by a Suddaine
approach of the Enemy I conceive it absolutely necessary that you forthwith send
out your Warrants for the raising of the Horse and ffoot within your severall Divisions and to order them to march to such places of the Coast were there may be
the greatest apprehention of danger and I desire you will give yourselves the
trouble to meet me at Sleaford on Saturday morning next were we may advise
together what may be best for his Majesties service and the safety of this County.
Grimsthorp Thursday Morning
at 3 of the Clock, 13 June 1667

Your very affectionate Friend
Lindsey

Though I never yet received a Letter from the Lords of the Counsell for a Lyst of
the severall Troopes and Companies with the names of the Officers yet by the
Postscript of the inclosed you will find it is required, therefore I desire you to
meet me so prepared that I may returne to their Lordships a satisfactory accompt.

[p. 130]

63. The Resolutions of the Lord Lieutenant and Deputy Lieutenants

Sleaford the 15 of June 1667

Resolved   That the Militia Captaine of Horse may have liberty to fitt up their
Troopes to four score by Volunteers.

Resolved   And it is desired that the Lord Lieutenant may write to the Counsel to desire answer whyther the Received Volunteers be admitted into his Majesties pay.

It is desired that the Lord Lieutenant will call into his owne hands the 4th part of the monthes Tax from Mr Thornton.

Resolved   That the Deputy Lieutenants of Lindsey do order the payment of a 4th part of a Monthes Tax for the year 1667 with all arrears due for any time past to be paid to Sir John Munson for Spittle Sessions, Charles Dymock Esquire for Horncastle, Sir Mathew Lister for Louth, Charles Pellum Esquire for Castor and Henry ffines Esquire for the City of Lincolne.

Resolved   That the Deputy Lieutenants shall have power to command the Post to send away any dispatches and that the Post Master to be paid out of the Weekes Tax.

Resolved   That my Lord Lieutenant will be pleased to send 6 Barrells of powder with match and bullett proportionable to Boston.

It is desired that my Lord Lieutenant do write to the Secretary that in this Emergencie he may have power to issue out Comissions for Volunteers and in case it be thought fitt and necessary to raise the Country by the Posse Comitatus and that he may have power to issue out Commissions and forme them into discipline.

Resolved   That the 6 Barrells of powder at Louth be carried to Saltfleet Haven with ammunition proportionable and the 4 Barrels at Lincolne be carried to Borough with ammunition proportionable with all the fixed Armes as well Musquets as Pikes.

Resolved   That the Companyes of ffoot of Sir Henry Herons Regiment be Quartered at Boston (viz) Sir Henry Heron and Captain Cardinall and Lieutenant Captain Thoryes and Sir Anthony Oldfeilds Troop of Horse, Captain Oldfeild at Sutton and Holbech and the other two Companyes between Boston and Wainfleet.

Resolved   That Sir Philip Tyrwits Troop of Horse be quartered at Saltfleet Haven.

Resolved   That 2 Companyes of ffoot of Sir Henry Bellasis Regiment be quartered at Grimsby vizt Captain Broxolme and Captain Booth.

Resolved   That Sir John Munsons Troop be quartered at Grimsby; Captain Thorolds Troop at Wainffleet and Captain Bolls his Troop at Borough, Mumby Chapple and Inomills and Captain Hydes Troop at Holbeach and Sutton.

Resolved   That Sir Henry Bellasis own Troop and Captain Sandersons Quartered at Saltfleet Haven and the Townes adjacent and the other 4 Companies to quarter between Northsummer coates and Grimsby.

Resolved   That Sir Thomas Meres Company be quartered at Grimsborough.

Resolved   That Sir John Newtons Regiment be quartered between Wainflleet and Throdlethorpe and that they may have libertie to quarter at any adjacent Towne which are not taken up for any other Quartor.

It is ordered that the severall Troopes and Regiments of ffoot do march from their Posts to their quarters were they shall be appointed.

That every Troop shall have one Horseman in their Quarters that may carry Intelligence to the nearest quartor.

Resolved   That all defaulters be immediately fined and the fines levied and disposed off according to his Majesties Instructions.

Resolved   That the Warrants that are issued out for the raising of the Militia mention 14 dayes pay.

[pp. 134–35]

64. The Counsells letter to the Lord Lieutenant 25 June 1667

After our very hearty Commendations to your Lordships, Whereas by severall Letters lately written from this Board by his Majesties especiall Command we have given direction for the drawing together of the County fforces of our Lieutenancies in order to the repelling any attempts the Enemy might make now in the time of soe apparant danger. And wheras the Enemy hath now really and actually invaded his Majesties Kingdome and burnt some of his Ships in the River Medway and doth still with a powerfull Navall fforce threaten other parts of this Kingdome, We are now to acquaint you that his Majestie in his great prudence and tender care is by all meanes possible and with all speed providing for the Ease and Safety of his loving Subjects not onely for the raising of an Army for the defence of the Kingdome and the reliefe of the standing Militia but onely in procureing mony for the support of the fforces to be imployed to that end ; but since it can not be reasonably imagined that a sufficient fforce can in short time be drawn together, or that his Majesty can be able for the present to support and pay the trained Bands whose attendance is necessary for the defence of your County untill other fforces can be drawn together, which if they should not doe the whole Country must be exposed to the Rapine of suche numbers (how small soever) as shall venture to land out of their Ships, we do very heartily recommend it to you, to call together the Justices of the Peace and other chief Gentlemen of the Country, who together with yourselves are to consider of the best wayes and meanes of the supporting those of the Militia who are necessary to look to the defence of the Country untill his Majesties forces can be drawn together with the least prejudice to the Country, and with every charge the Country under goes his Majesty will be ready to concurr in and advance all due wayes and meanes for your reparation and satisfaction not doubting but as good Patriots you will with all possible alacrity and dilligence comply with this his Majesties desire.

We bid you Lordship farewell from the Court at Whytehall 25 June 1667.

Your very loving Friends

Manchester, Craven Bridgwater, Thomas Ingram, Arlington, Fitzharding, Thomas Clifford, William Morrice, Richard Browne[1]

Received this from Sir William Thorold by my own way Thursday between 12 and 1 of the clocke June 27.[2]

[p. 136]

[1]   The letter is signed by Browne.

[2]   This is written at the side of the letter.

65. [The Earl of Lindsey to the Deputy Lieutenants.]

My Lord Lieutenant to the Deputy Lieutenants.

Gentlemen,

Having Received this inclosed[1] from the Lords of the Counsell, I have sent this

Messenger purposely to you that you may put in Execution their Lordships desires. I supose a Generall meeting will be absolutely necessary at Lincoln where I would be present myself, but my Wives extraordinary ilness preventeth me who am

Your very Affectionate Friend
Lindsey

Grimsthorp June 29
at 2 of the Clock in the morning.

[p. 137]
1 Cf. OB 64.

66. The Deputy Lieutenants letter to my Lord

My Honoured Lord
In obedience to your Lordships Commands and those of His Majesties most Honourable Privy Counsell, We have this day mett at Lincolne but the Summons was as Generall as we could make it to the Justices and Gentlemen of this County in soe short a time before the 14 dayes duty were expired; there hath few Gentlemen appeared and of our selves we are not able to undertake anything for the whole County, though to our powers and fortunes we should decline nothing of service to his Majesty, but find the Country is not able for any time to maintaine their Militia they have been soe exhausted by payment and the mony charged out in specie as ther is little left to make Markets, there being no Manufactors in this Country to bring in any Returnes, yet we have thought fitt with submission to your Lordships pleasure in it to appoint such a constant Guard against little incursions of the Enemyes as we may make good for some time out of our Militia, and if it be thought too little we most humbly desire his Majesties to increase it from the Inland adjacent Counties whose Militias are discharged from all duty but the particulars of the Resolutions you will receive hear inclosed which is all but we are.

[p. 137]

67. Resolved at Lincolne by the Deputy Lieutenants at a Generall meeting on the 29 of June 1667.

Resolved   That 2 Companyes of ffoot and one Troop of Horse be kept upon duty and no more for 7 dayes and soe succesively.
Resolved   That the Horse do quartor at Saltfleet Haven.
Resolved   That the Companies of Sir Henry Bellasis Regiment do quartor at Grimsby successively.
Resolved   That the Companies of the Regiment of Sir John Newton and Sir Henry Heron do quartor at Burgh in the Marsh.
Resolved   That Sir John Munsons Troop do march on Munday next to Saltfleet Haven.
Resolved   That Sir Henry Bellasis Regiment do begin with one Company on Munday next to keep guard at Grimsby and so successively till further order.
Resolved   That Sir John Newtons Regiment begin with one Company on

Munday next to keep Guard at Burgh and so successively until further order.

Resolved   That Sir Henry Herons Regiment do releive Sir John Newtons at the same place in the same order.

Resolved   That Captain Thorolds Troop do march to Saltfleet Haven on Munday morning beginning 8 of July to do duty likewise for 7 dayes and that he be relieved by Sir Philip Tirwit July 15 then by Sir Anthony Oldfeild July 22 then by Captain Hyde July 29 then by Captain Bolls August the 5 who is reserved to the last his Troop, Having done duty 14 dayes last year and no other Troop.

Resolved   That the rest of the Militia be dismist forthwith with Command to be in readynes to march to their respective Guards at an houres warning.

Resolved   That the Ammunition sent from the Magazine at Lincoln be delivered over to him that shall command the Guard successively without diminution.

Resolved   That the fixt Musquets at the Magazine be forthwith sent to Grimsby.

Resolved   That Warrants do issue to require the Arms finders to supply the Souldiers for 7 dayes pay and ammunition propotionable as they shall come uppon duty and that the Foot have but 12d a day for pay onely.

Resolved   That my Lord Lieutenant be desired to give order for the payment of the Officers as well comissionated as not comissionate and also for some Sallery for the Clarkes who be at extraordinary paines.

Sir John Monson senior	Sir John Monson junior
Sir Philip Tyrwhit	Sir William Hickman
Sir Robert Markham	Sir Edward Rossiter
Sir Henry Bellasis	Sir Edward Ayscough
Sir William Wray	Charles Dymock
Charles Pelham Esquire	

[pp. 137–38]

68. [The King to the Earl of Lindsey]

Charles Rex, 29 June 1667 in the 19 yeare of our Reigne

Right Trusty and Right well beloved Cousin and Counsellor, Wee greet you well. Whereas the insolent Spirit of our Enemies hath prevailed soe far with them as to make an Invasion uppon this our Kingdome which is in continuall danger of their attempts uppon the same, Wee hold our selves obliged to use all fitt and proper meanes both for the repelling of our said Enemies and the defence of our People, which as it can not be better nor (As we conceive) otherwise done then by the speedy raising of a Considerable Army, so neither can that be performed without good summes of money. Wee therefore relieing uppon your wisdome and readiness to asist us and your Country in this Exigent have thought fitt to recommend the effectuall consideration thereof unto you to require your utmost endeavour forthwith to dispose and quicken all our Loyall Subjects within your Lieutenancy that are in capascity of lending to make a voluntary liberal advance of what summes of mony they can afford by way of loane towards the supply of our pressing occasions in this time of publike danger to be repayd them againe out of the the 16 Monthes Assessment in course. We will not doubt but that your endeavour which we assure orselves you will engage to the utmost will meet with so much loyalty and prudence in them as easily to advance what we reasonbly expect, a speedy and cheerfull complyance with our necessities in this so important a juncture of affaires and soe we bid you heartily farewell. Given at our Court at Whyte hall the 29 of June 1667 In The 19 year of our Reigne

By his Majesties Command
William Morrice

[pp. 139–40]

69. [The Earl of Lindsey to the Deputy Lieutenants]

Gentlemen

   Having Received a Letter from his Majestie a Coppy whereof I have sent you hear inclosed, Commanding me to the utmost of my endeavers fforthwith to dispose and quicken all his Majesties loyall subjects within my Lieutenancy that are in a capasity of lending to make a voluntary and liberall advance of what summes of mony they can afford by way of a Loane towards the supply of his Majesties pressing occasions in this time of publique danger, I desire the favour of your meeting with me at the Angell in Sleaford upon Tuesday the 9th of this instant July by 10 of the Clock in the forenoon and that in the interim you would communicate the inclosed to all persons that are capassitated for lending. I cannot doubt but when we meet I shall find a speedy and cheerful complyance with his Majesties necessityes and that this whole County according to its abillity will be as foreward as any other what ever, to express its duty and loyalty uppon every occasion. I am

Gentlemen
Your very affectionate Friend
Lindsey

Grimthorpe
July 1 1667

[p. 139]

70. [The Earl of Lindsey to the King]

The Lord of Lindseys Answer

In obedience to his Majesties Command I have this day met with my Deputy Lieutenants and other Justices and Gentlemen who in their Several parts of this County have been active in endeavering to borough mony by way of advance uppon the 11 Monthes Tax for Soe important an occacion as the paying of the Army His Majesty has thought fit to raise for his necessary defence and preservation of his people and Kingdome against his Enemy. But truely without success as no mony is to be gotten, though all profess both their loyalties and selfe interest as English men would engage them to supply his Majestie if they either had or knew how to borough any in this County which is now reduced to those great necessities as ther is not mony left in it to make markets with (they have been soe exhausted by payments and the carrying it out by specie), nor is ther any manufacture, Mine or other meanes to bring in any by returnes, as in other parts of this Kingdome, soe as no Comodity yeilds any price, Tenents breake, and the Gentry get little or noe Rents (though they have the misfortune as a meritane

County to be under the greater duty with their Militia and payments and most others). Yet if ther be mony to be gotten at London upon their Securityes they are ready Severally to be bound for it, in a proprtion to any other County, If the necessity continues, or in case of any actuall Invasion to furnish and maintaine uppon their owne charge a considerable proportion of Horse for 6 Weekes to come, as an Addition to the forces of this County. All which I desire you will humbly Represent from me to his Majesty who with his Deputy Lieutenats neither have nor will be failing to their power in anything for his Majesties service.[1]

[pp. 140–41]
[1] Another copy of this letter can be found in LA, 10 Anc., Lot 355/1.

71. To the Right Honorable Robert Earl of Lindsey Great Chamberlaine of England Lord Lieutenant of the County of Lincoln and one of His majesties Honourable Privy Counsell

Whitehall, August 13 1667

To be left with the Postmaster at Sleaford.
My Lord,
    Yesterday I received your Lordships Letter and forthwith moved his Majesty concerning the matter therein contained, who gave me command to signife his pleasure unto your Lordship that upon the receipt hereof you proceed immediately to the dischargeing of the Militia Troop and Companyes of your Lieutenancy and send them to their severall homes, which is all at present from
                    My Lord
                        Your Lordships most humble servant
                            William Morrice
[p. 142]

72. To Sir Henry Heron, Sir Anthony Oldfeild, and Charles Dymocke Esquire.

Gentlemen,
    By his Majesties Command to me in a letter from Mr Secretary Morrice bearing date the 13th of this instant a Coppy whereof You have heare sent inclosed, You are forthwith to discharge all Troopes and Companies of the Militia now uppon duty at any place upon the Sea coast or else where and to send them to their severall homes, soe not doubting of your care in the speedy Execution of the same I remaine
    Your very affectionate Friend
    Lindsey
Grimsthorpe, August 15 1667.
You are to bring of the severall ammunition and Armes with your guards where there are any and place them in the usual storehouse for that purpose. I desire to receive an account from you of the severall Fines charged and levied uppon all defaulters both of Horse and Foot.

[p. 142]

73.

5 of November 1667

Received of Sir Anthony Oldfield of Spalding Bart by the order of
Mr Edmond Ashley of Gedny the sum of four pounds four shillings which was
due unto him for 14 dayes duty at Boston   04 04 00
I say received By me Thomas Gibson

[p. 267]

APPENDIX ONE

TAXATION AND LOCAL GOVERNMENT

74. The Earle of Southampton and my Lord Ashleys Letter to Sir Anthony Oldfeild Bart High Sherriff for the Countie of Lincolne.

After our heartie commendations, Wee doe hereby recommend to your care the Assessing and levieing of the 12 hundred three score thousand pounds granted to his Majestie by the late Act of Parliament[1] and your proceeding therein according as yow are impowred and directed by the said Act, which we herewith transmit to you, And the Coppie of his Majesties order to us to appoint the Sherriffs to bee General Receavers, whereof wee have directed our letters and instructions to them to pay in the monyes which wee presse uppon them to be speedilie performed in respect of the publique Service. Those monyes are by His Majesty designed for and in respect if the payment be delayed the least inconvenience that arises hereby will be His Majestie paying Interest for the publique concerne. And that which concerns the generall good is soe involved therein that if any quarterly payment be delayed the rest will hinder the credit whereby we so ryase ourselves. And therefore we pray you to contribute all your endeavers to the speedy return of these monyes as that wherein all our concernes will be found and your care herein shall be represented to His Majestie and acknowledged to you

Your verie Loveing friends
Southampton
Ashly

18 January 1662

[p. 1]
1 13 Charles II st.2, c.3, which aimed to raise £1,260,000.

75. To our very loving friends the Commissioners in the Countie of Lincolne

After our heary Comendations, the supplie of his Majesties publike affaires being now reduced into the antient way of Subsidies[1] and most of his Majesties subjects having been by long disuse much unaccquainted with the nature of Subsidies and their proceedings thereon, we have thought fit to recommend unto you this important business desiring you to make it so well understood as that all persons may know (that though it be a Tax of 4/- of the lands and 2s 8d goods) yet men have not been ordinarily taxed at about the twentyth parte of the yearly value of their Lands and so proportionately for their goods which, as it can little presse on any that is to pay it, soe unlesse it be duely assessed on the behalfe of the Crowne

the product of it will noe wayes answear the occasions it was given for; and
therefore we that are accquainted with those occations pray you to consider how
important the reasons were that induced the two houses of Parliament to grant
those Subsidies and to make the same a Motive to yourselves to use all expediton
and dilligence in the Execution of the service and to be very careful in giving
order for the due assessing the same, the yearly value of the Lands be generally
improved by inclosures, disparking, drayning, ffloteing and other Husbandry
above the proportion that it did hereto fore bear, and that care be taken that sufficient persons be named Collectors and such as can give securety suetable to the
quality of their Collection; and because there hath been great abuses formerly,
the men living in one place where they have small estates and geting themselves
Assessed there, the Commissioners not having duly considered what they
possessed either in the parts of that Countie or in other Countryes, we pray you to
be carefull therefore that noe evasions of that kind may prejudice the Service; and
this rule which we find in all former Instructions given from the Borde upon this
occation, Wee recommend unto you that noe Commissioner of the subsidies or
Justice of the Peace whome the Lawe requires to have twenty pounds per annum
in Lands be set under that summe and when those of best possessions highten
themselves every one else will more cheerfully bear their proportions and by this
meanes the tax by Subsidies will recover his valuation which being falne to soe
low a Summ was by the late Usurpers laid aside. This proceeding will give the
best proof of your affections and his Majestie has reason to give you thankes for
the fruit of your endeaver which may prevent the subtilty of others who ayme to
lessen the supplies for publike occations or a meanes to make all things revert to
the late confusions as a probable way to advance this service. We recommend
unto you that some of the commissioners that are best experienced in that service
may be appointed to take care of the severall Divisions assigned to them and
uppon the whole matter that it be performed with suche Judgment and equitie
that the charge may be borne with chearfullness and paid with readines and the
good temper of the Nation may the better be preserved therby. And soe we bid
you heartily farwell

From the Court at Whitehall

14 August 1663
Clarendon, Albermale, Manchester, Carberry, Gilbert London, Charles Berkley,
Thomas Southampton, Barkshire, John Backley, Bath, Ashley, George Carterett,
Middleton, William Compton, William Morrice, St Albans, Henry Bennett.

[pp. 48–50]
[1] 15 Charles II c.9.

76.

August 18 1663
This day the Commissioners for Assessing the four Subsidies met at the Angell in
the Baylie of Lincolne.

Resolved   That Noe man of £1000 per annum Real estate shall be charged
             above the rate of £20 in the Kings books and soe proportionatelly to a
             greater or lesser Estate as well Real as personall.

Resolved   That every twelve thousand pounds personall estate be charged equall with £ 1000 per annum Reall and so proportionably to a greater or lesser Estate.

Lincolne, Holland
To the Chiefe Constable of the Wapentake of   [1] and to every of them

Wheras we are impowred by an Act made the last session of this present Parliament for the granting to his Majestie four entire subsidies by the Temporallity. These are therefore in pursuance thereof to will and require you to summons thre or more of the ablest persons of Estates within each Parish and Towne shipp within your severall Divisions to appeare before us or some of us at   [1] The   [1] Day of September next then and there to receive such Directions for the assessing and Taxing the first two of the four Subsidies granted to his Majestie aforesaid as by the said Act we are impowered and that you yourselves doe allsoe appeare before us at the day and place aforesaid with this precept and a lyst of Persons Soe by you summoned, wherof faile not as you will answer the contrary at your perills. Given under our hands and Seales this   [1] Day of August in the XV yeare of the reign of our Soveraigne Lord King Charles the second Anno Domini 1663.

[pp. 50–51]
[1] The manuscript has been left blank at these points.

77. [From the Earl of Southampton and Lord Ashley to the Commissioners for the poll tax]

To the Commissioners within the County of Lincoln

All our hearty Commendations etc. Wee haveing sent down unto you the 2 Acts for rayseing mony by a Poll[1] and other wise towards the maintenance of the present Warr together with 3 printed warrants, One to the Assessors, another to the Subcollectors and a third to the High Collectors, we have great reason to believe will contribute much to your ease and dispatch and therefore we have little to add because the particular Directions concerning your selves as Commissioners are so expressly set downe in those Acts and when we consider unto what service the monyes levyable thereby are appointed and how the product of those Bills was estimated at the House of Commons £500,000 in ease of the Land Taxes. We think it our duty to intimate unto you that if the same be not carefully and industriously performed this Sumers expedition at Sea, on which the safety of this Nation so much depends, will suffer much thereby. And therefore that His Majesty will expect accordingly to the powers given by the acts that you examine the presenters return of the Assessment, that no persons charged may be exempted but that all names be returned in the first Assessment or estreat and every one justly charged accordingly to the rates set uppon them for their severall Capasityes in the Act and that all the defaulters uppon whome no distress can be found be carefully returned into the Exchequer and if you find any person formerly residing amonge you shifting their abodes to conceale their payments so that you cannot well meet with them that you give some notice to us thereof that we may commit it to some bodyes care to make enquiry after them. We doubt not likewise that you will call upon the Collectors and the Receivers Generall to make their payment according to the times of the Acts and perform any thing else that may advance and conduce to this important affaire and soe bidding you heartily farewell we rest

Your very loveing Friends
T. Southampton, Ashley

Southampton House
February 6 1667

[p. 125]
[1] 18/19 Charles II, c.1.

78.

Lincoln, February 14 1667

The Comissioners for the Poll mony met this day at the Angell in the Bayle of Lincoln being the usual place of meeting and agreed to subdivide thesmselves and others there present for the Execution of this Act into the Respective Sessons hundreds and Libertyes in which they are resident, And to issue out warrants accordingly. It is desired that the said absent Comissioners will put the said Act in execution within their respective precincts according to the severall powers and times therin listed.

The warrant then agreed upon to the Chief Constables.
Whereas by an Act of Parliament entitled an Act for the raiseing of monyes by a Poll and other wise towards the maintenance of the present Warr, We amongst others are appointed Comissioners for levieing the sum. These are to require You to issue out your Warrants to two of the ablest inhabitants of every parish within your respective Divisions strictly charging and commanding them to appeare before the Commissioners at the [1] uppon the [1] of this instant February by the [1] of the Clock in the [1] noon then and there to receive Directions for the rateing and Assessing of the said Moneys. Hereof neither you nor they are to faile.

[p. 126]
[1] The manuscript has been left blank at these points.

79. A Letter to Sir Phillip Warwick.

Sir,

According to the Directions of an Act of the Poll Bill we have this day met, but noe Acts or Instructions being sent into the Countryes, We whose names are hear subscribed are all the Comissioners that have appeared yet to carry on the busines for his Majesties Service with all the vigour and expedition. We have agreed of a Forme for our Warrants and Subdivided ourselves and the rest of the Comissioners as the Act Directs but untill Acts come and are disposed to the severall Comissioners (which we desire for Expedition may be done by the High Sherrif) The Service will be much obstructed though we shall be faileing to nothing to our duties which is all but that we are Sir

Your humble servants

Thomas Hadney, Mayor, John Munson, John Munson, William Brogdine, S. Richier, Henry Morley, Stephen Mason, Richard Wetherall, Richard Milner, Henry Morley.

The Parishes and Commissioners for this County are very numerous and therefore your Acts and Warrants Accordingly.

[p. 126]

80. To the Right Worshipfull His Majesties Justices of the Peace for the Division of Holland, County of Lincoln.

Whereas it pleased his Majesties Justices of the Peace at Sleaford session on [1] July last to make these following propositions for us the ffarmers of the Hearth mony for the County of Lincolne of our part to perform and observe, which done they would encourage and promote the collecting the said revenew ariseing to his Majestie by ffire Hearths and Stoves in the County by Constables and the paying of it by them to us or Deputy at such place as wee from time to time shall appoint, These are therfore to testify your Worships that we do consent and agree to severall propositions then made and do promise for ourselves and all our Deputy Officers to perform the same.

And first we are willing and do consent that the Constables at present until we have made our view do gather the old Duplycates and do promise that no harme shall come uppon the Constables for any short returne, If afterwards uppon our view there be found more Chimnys than hath been returned.

2   After we have made a view we do promise to fix a Scedule to our Warrant or Duplycates for allowing the Constables to gather by.

3   In our Warrants or Duplicates for Collecting the Retinew Wee doe and will impoure the severall Constables to give accquittance for all such monyes as they shall receive which aquittances we allow of to be a sufficient discharge for soe much monyes to the parties who at any time shall produce the same.

4   If at any time the Constables shall return to us any person in arrears and unpaid we do promise to make a Second demand at the house of suche persons soe returned and give them a convenient time before we distreine for the duty.

5   We do promise to allow the Constables 3d in the pound for the Sallerie in gathering it as was then propounded.

6   If at any time it shall so happen that any of our under Officers shall distreine any person who by reason of his povertye is exempted from paying the said duty without first giving him a convenient time to provide for himselfe of a Certficate for his exemption, in such case we do not onely promise to restore to the partie his goods but also to allow him necessary charges according as anyone of your Worships shall deem or think fitt, but if we give them a days time or two to provide themselves of Certificates and they wll not, Wee hope your Worships will not blame us for distreining them because it is impossible for us to know the povertie of such persons without your Worships Certificate neither doth the Act provide any other way for their Exemption to all this.

Witness our hands the 19 day of September 1667

Edward Copley
William Batte

[pp. 262–63]
[1] The day of the month is not stated.

81.

At the general Quartor Sessions of the Peace houlden at Saplding in the part and the county aforesaid the 10 of January in the 18 year of the Raigne of our Sovereign Lord King Charles the second over England etc. before Sir Anthony Oldfeild Barronet, Henry Bussee and John Humphry Esquire, his Majesties Justices of the Peace within the part of the County aforesaid amongst others assigned.

Wheras it appeareth to the Court by the Petition of diverse of the Chiefe Inhabitants of the Charge bearers of Spalding and Pinchbeck that the severall Highwayes in and about the Towneships and Parishes and Precincts and Libertyes thereof are of late yeares and at this time gone into very great decay and ruine to the great danger of Travellers and passengers and hazard of their goods, Chattells and carriages and the manifest decay of Trade and Traffique unto their Townes and places, and that theres no hopes or expectation they will ever be well and effectually repayred and amended in and by the ordinary way and course of Common Minworkes or Boone dayes those dayes works ar for the most part slightly performed and yet with muche expense to the said Townes and wheras the Court is Certified and well assured that by antient use and custome of these Townes every Cottager and Laborer in the said Townes shall every year pay 12 pence a peece for and towards the repayre of the high wayes there in lieu of their 6 boon dayes worke, and every subsidie man according to £5 in goods and 40/- in land not chargeable to the high ways by other statutes and meanes shall pay 2/- a yeare to the Overseers of the High wayes in lieu of 2 able men to labor in the repayre of the high wayes uppon those 6 dayes, which by long and muche experience have been found and proved to be both of farr better use for the repayre of the high wayes then the finding and sending out of Labour as the manner in other places is, and soe prayed the Judgement and order of the Courts for remedie and reliefe in this behalfe. It is therefore ordered by the Court that this said good old and antient use and custome of the said Towne shall be and stand henceforth revewed and revived, and that every the Laborers and Cottagers and Subsidy men aforesaid shall once every year, that is to say between Easter and Whitsuntide, pay their proportion of mony into the handes of the Surveyors of the high wayes, that is to say every Cottager and Laborer 12d and every Subsidyman as aforesaid 2/- for and towards the repayreing and amending all and every the severall defective high wayes of the said Townes uppon paine of being presented and Indicted in the Sessions for their contempt and disobedience against this order, and uppon collection and receipt of these moneys the overseers of the highwayes are carefully from time to time to see and cause the highwayes to be repayred and ammended therwith and to make a due accompt of the disburseing and laying out of the same for the use and wherof aforesaid as they will answer the contrary at their perills; provided that this order shall not extend nor be intended to obstruct and hinder anyones Charity and free good will and in sending help and Ayd and other voluntary and necessary contributions towards the repayring of the high wayes but have invitation and due encouragement there.

p. Charles Rushworth

[pp. 237–38]

APPENDIX TWO

ECCLESIASTICAL DISPUTES AT SPALDING

82. To the Bishop of Lincoln[1]

May it please your Honour,

Att the request of Mr Styles Minister of Croyland I could doe noe lesse then ceritife the truth, That Florence Mason swore desperately against the said Mr Styles, that Hee and others committed a Ryot into the Vicaridge house, where upon the Under Clerke of the Peace granted out Warrants of good behaviour against him and others, neither I nor any of the Justices knowing of it. Thus I make bold to certifie your Honour that you may have no prejudicate oppinion against this Bearer Mr William Styles and Soe I rest

Your most dutiful Servant

To be commanded whilst

Anthony Oldfeild

[p. 7]
1 Robert Sanderson, consecrated 28 October 1660.

83. To the Bishop of Lincolne

My Lord,

About halfe a year agoe your Lord ship received some Information (concerning Mr Robert Peirson Minister of Spalding) from severall Inhabitants of the said Towne, as well as from divers Justices of the Peace in the parts adjacent. Their desires to your Lord=ship then weare that hee might not be Lycensed by your Honour soe as to be the settled Minister in Spalding, partly for that he was not presented to the Liveing according to the true intent and meaning of the particular Instrument in that case made and provided, as allsoe because he would not receive Episcopall Ordination and conforme to the Lyturgy and Discipline of the Church (to the observance of both which the said Instrument doth particularly enjoyne him) but especially for that they humbly conceave a person of soe knowne factious principles (as he all alonge has been) was alltogether unfitt to be continued in such a ffactious Towne and parts as Spalding, and the Neighbouring Country, hath been and to this day are. Uppon the very same score it is that wee now againe presume to interrupt your Lord-shipp humbly craveing that hee may not receive any Lycence or Confirmation (as to this Place) Till your Lordshipp shall have such satisfaction from him as in your Wisedome may be accepted off, he being still guilty of all which we formerly laid to his charge, And (if we mistake not) addes to them dayly many and great aggravations; for whereas he promised to take holy Orders and Conforme, at his comeing home, he said there was noe need for his so doeing, And denied that he had taken any; but now since the Act of Conformite[1] came forth hee gives out that a Scotch Bishopp[2] (of the Orcades they say) ordained him about February last, notwithstanding which he hath since refused to bury our dead; Hee Baptises Children privately (and that within these three dayes) without the Signe of the Crosse; And that little of the service which he doth aford us on a Sunday Morning (for in the after noon we have nothing but the Lords=Prayer and an Hymne neither Catechiseing etc., nor any notice is taken of the Churches Festivals) is performed soe perfunctorily, by peice mease and with soe many Hysteron proterons (As wee may terme it) as if it were on purpose to render it ridiculus to all that here it. In his Extemporary prayers before Sermons he never takes notice of the King as head or Govenor of the Church nor of the Bishops (imitateing wee presume those which King James takes notice of in the Hampton Court Conference)[3] nor Universities. Nay, when the late Act for Conformity was even passed he made it his business for two or three Sundayes to preache downe Conformity (as we conceave) under the notion of formall worshipp, denounceing a ffamine of the word from the words of the Prophet Amos 8:11.[4] Now if these and the like be not infallible tokens whereby to know a man given to Sedition, we most humbly crave your Lordships pardon, Our Zeale to our Common Mother the Church being the sole prompter of such kinds of Information, which we are put uppon the more because Hee vaunts it among his Complices that Spalding Minister is totally exempted from Episcoppall Jurisdiction, but we hope your Lordshps will judge the Contrary, and yet grant him no manner of Lycence till some satisfaction in the premise be given to

Your Lordships humble servants
A. O., E. S., J. B., etc

[pp. 9–11]

[1] The Act of Uniformity, 14 Charles II c.4, passed in May 1662.

[2] Thomas Sydserf, Bishop of Galloway, who became Bishop of Orkney in November 1661.

[3] Presumably 'No Bishop no King'.

[4] 'Behold, the days come saith the Lord God, that I will send a famine in the land, not a famine of bread, nor a thirst for water but of hearing the words of our Lord', Amos 8:11.

84. To Mr Lawson at Linconle

Mr Lawson,

I have sent you Articles to bee exhibited against Mr Peirson and would desire you to draw them into form to our best advantage. I have waved all those which concerne Title, and severall other materiall ones relating to the late Act of Uniformity[1] and other matters as conceaving here may be ennough to venture at present, but with an intent to prosecute the rest in case hee should have the good fortune to cleare himself of these. Pray Sir let nothing be wanting for the Carrieing on of the busines, for the eleventh Article itself is so true that the verie proveing of that one Article will I hope much fecilitate the clearing up of our Evidence. If any article be expected against our Church=wardens pray exhibite this (viz) That since the Action was entred they have behaved themselves as irreverently in the Church as formerly, never kneeling at any part of Service, nor standing up when the Churche Commands and in generall Irreverent and disorderly they are in soe high a manner that there might Articles Sans number be preferrd against them and especially John Dale, but that is not worth ones labour to doe it considering that Dales encouragements are so great that hee told me He could goe further for iid then we could for 20/- and that when I and the rest had done our worst it should not cost him ten groates more then his rideing charges.

Yours
Anthony Oldfeild

[pp. 11–13]

[1] 14 Charles II c.4

85. Articles exhibited at Lincoln against Mr Robert Peirson

1   In, or about, January 1657 Matthew Attkinson of Spalding desired this Mr Robert Peirson to Christen his Child; what, sayes he, I will warrant you would have Godfathers and God mothers; ey, replyes the ffather, If I might; well, sayes Mr Peirson, goe your way for the child will be as well unchristened as Christened; and refused absolutely to baptize it.

2   In September or there about 1658 Robert Scot of Spalding desired Mr Peirson to Christen his child, hee haveing had eleven Children baptized before that time in the same Parish. Mr Peirson did then absolutely refuse to baptize it and told him allsoe that his Child would be as well unbaptized as baptized.

3   Much about the same time or about the year 1659, Hee did very frequently Preach, speake and declare in derogation of the Booke of Common Prayer in Spalding Church. He hath compared it to Heathen writters and has told us severall time that the very first Sentence in it (At which time soe ever a Sinner) was a lye and Anti=scripturall; that to have the very name of God ffather and God mother amongst Christians was next to blasphemy; all this will be sworne by divers credible persons.

4   Much about the said time (for he cannot speake to a sett day or month there being then little hope that any honest man should ever dare to talk of such like passages) being discourseing with Mr Thomas Pickard curate of Whapleade Drove, He Mr Pei[r]son possitively asserted that the greatest causes of our late troubles were a Popish Lytergy and Antichristian Bishops.

5   As much as in him lay he hindered the Kings Restoration and the election of a free Parliament, for being desired in or about February 1660 To publise and subscribe the Lincolnshire Declaration for a fre Parliament[1] he refused both and tould Mr Thomas Wallet the Chief Constable (who brought it to him) that if the King was there present and Commanded him yet he would not doe it; nay if the Parliament should command it he would not obey their Command. And the said Mr Wallet was tould by Mr Philip Jolly that Mr Peirson and some others did pittie Mr Wallets case very much, and said I would doe well for him if he came off whith the losse of his Estate for offering to promote suche a designe as that was.

6   He continued a better of Schisme by keeping up his gathered Church (as they called it) long after this wherein He the said Mr Peirson together with one Mr Scheldricke of Wisbith,[2] Robert Vigerous Apothecary, John Bumford Trauslatour and others of Spalding and the Neighbouring parts had combined themselves into a Brotherhood directly contrary to the Canon of King James; And he hath appointed and be present at publique and private meetings for Sermons without direction or Lycence of the Bishop of the Dyocese Contra Canons 72, 73 et 12.

7   He administered the Sacrament of the Lords Supper, after his absurd fashion to his selected crew, before he had received any Orders at all which wee ever heard off.

8   Long after the Act of Oblivion was come forth (viz.) in August 1660,[3] Hee refused to use the Booke of Common Prayer when Mr William Wragg one of the Church wardens bought it and Sent it to him with a Letter by the Sexton in be

halfe of the Towne, Mr Peirson sending him word by John Catell of Spalding that he might as well have offered him Lawne sleeves as that boake, and notwithstanding then was a new Font set up, the said Mr Peirson would not use it but Christned at the Deske with a Basin which when the said Mr Wragg had taken away about December 1661 Mr Peirson brought a Basin of his owne and made use thereof.

9   In the year 1659 and 1660 He sould soe much stone appertaineing to the ffabricke of the Chancell as he Receive £1 5s 0d for, of William Piggit, and about the same time built up a Cribbe at the Chancell dore (the Cribbe adjoyneing to the wall) where he fodered his Cowes (or Kime) for a long while.

10   That long time since the Act of Oblivion passed, nay since the consecration of our Lord Bishop,[4] this Mr Peirson together with Thomas Welby gent, Israel Jackson gent and diverse others met together at Boston to consult uppon matters and courses to be taken by them tending to the deprovement of the Booke of Common Prayer and in particular to agree uppon a fitt way for adminstring of the Lords supper Contra Canone 73; we cannot now pitch uppon the precise time but if need be we will learn it out.

11   About March last he tooke Orders from a Scotch Bishop[5] without Letters demissory from his Right Reverend Diocesan who was at the same time in London, by virtue of which orders he preaches, reades etc., in the Parish Church of Spalding from March 1662 till almost the middle of August 1662. And all this before he had first consented and subscribed to the 3 Articles (mentioned in the 36 Canon of King James) in the presence of the Bishop of the Dyocess (or Ordinery) wherein he preached etc. And this is not only against the 34 or 37 Canons but the matter of fact is likewise very true.

12   Since the time of his Ordination he hath denied his taking of orders, thereby keeping many of his Parish from the Communion who would gladly have been partakers of it and there by occasioning presentments against diverse of his Parishoners causelesly; this was a little before and after Easter last, as will be proved by John Barton gent. and severall others if need be.

13   In Easter weeke last he strenously asserted the legality and validity of Presbyterian Ordination, offered a disputation with Mr Nicholas East Vicar of Pinchbecke, told him he had 9 or 10 demonstrative arguments (amongst many others) to evince the truth therof, this Mr East hath given under his hand and will depose when called.

14   He hath since omitted to use the forme of Prayer and diverse of the Orders and Ceremonies prescribed in the Communion booke and Canons which will thus appeare.

15   At Easter last he administered the Lords Supper to such as did not kneele, contra Canon 27. And in particular to Christopher Blades, Christopher Murrell, John Cattell, Thomas Bladesmith, Thomas Gorrell, Mistress Moore the Wife of Joseph Moore Esquire, Mrs Ellen Jolly, Widdow Love, Katherine Cocke and Margaret Tavener.

16   He did not at the same time Receive the Communion himself contra Cannon 21.

17   He hath not formerly nor since Ordination declared the Kings Supremacy according to Canon the first.

18   He hath since refused to bury the dead who were not denounced e[x]communicated *Majori Excommunicatione* contra Canon 38, and in particular he refused to bury Ralph Wright on the 16 of April last and Elizabeth the Wife of Matthew Jackson and a Child of William Worrells on the 24 or 25 of Aprill last.

19   He hath ever neglected Catechizing both before and since his Ordination; Canon 59.

20   He hath ever neglected to give notice of Holydayes and ffasting dayes and that after Sir Edward Lake had admonished him in that very particular at the visitation of Boston; Canon 64.

21   He doth not give the accustomned reverence when the Lord Jesus is mentioned in the time of Divine Service; Canon 18.

22   He hath behaved himself rudely in the Church Contra Canon 11, and this by the hindering and interrupting the people in reading the Psalmes by standing at the Prayers of the Church when the Rubrick sayes he shall kneel. And all this hath been soe usual that a mistake cannot be easily made either in the matter or time, but particularly on the Sunday before St Bartholomhew last it being the next Lords day, after Sir Edward Lake granted him in a lycence.

23   He hath ever neglected the Celebration of Divine Service on holy dayes Contra Canon 13 and the Litany on Wednesdayes and ffrydayes; Canon 15.

24   He never tooke notice of the forme of Prayer to used by Preachers before their Sermon; Canon 55.

25   He hath neglected and refused to use all along the Booke of Common Prayer etc. in direct opposition to every word in the 14 Canon and against the Act of Parliament 1 Elizabeth c.2 which is confirmed by the Act of Uniformity 14 Charles II and after this late Act passed; for he would never read the whole service as it is appointed but once in 3 or 4 Lords day the Litany without any of the second service, sometimes the Commandments without either Litany, Epistle or Gospell, and sometimes the Epistle and Gospell without either Litany or Commandments. In the afternoon he never read the confession and absolution nor those other Prayers and Collects which the Church appoints but hurried all things over to get into the Pulpit contrary to the 14th Canon.

26   In June last or as soon as the Act of Uniformity came forth, He preaches uppon the Text Amos 8:11 for two Lords days if not more, disquieting the minds of the people with discourses about ffamine of the word and fformality in worship and did not cease doeing so till he was told of his great indiscretion by some of his Parishoners.

27   Since his Subscription before Sir Edward Lake He hath declared his dissent to the Doctrine contained in the new Common prayer booke, viz. uppon the 17, 18 or 16 August last, for being shewn that the Rubrike at the end of the Publique

Baptisme, where the Church sayes, It is certaine by Gods word that children who dye, being baptized, before they committ actuall sinne are undoubtedly saved, and asked what he said to it (his Judgement concerning the efficacy of Baptisme being well enough knowen to his whole Parish) or how he could subscribe thereto; his answer was that he subscribed and declared to the use of the Lyturgy not the Doctrine therein contained, whereas the Cry went before that it was the Discipline not the Doctrine which gave offence. Now if such evasion and mentall reservations be allowable we do not yet see why any man should refuse any manner of oath or other engagement for the Act requires the giveing of an unfeigned assent and consent to all things contained in the booke as well as to the use of all things in the Booke.

[pp. 13–18]
1 BL Egerton MS 2541, fo 362.
2 William Sheldrake, Lecturer at Wisbech: see A. G. Matthews, *Calamy Revised* (Oxford, 1934), 436–7.
3 12 Charles II c.11: An Act of free and general pardon indemnity and oblivion.
4 Sanderson was consecrated 28 October 1660.
5 Thomas Sydserf, Bishop of Orkney. Cf. OB 83.

86. To my Lord Bishop of Lincolne

My Lord,

About the 15th of the last month diverse of the Neighbours in Spalding had severall meetings towards the settling of this soe much divided Towne in Peace, at the last of which Mr Robert Peirson did under his hand and Seale resigne all his pretended title Interest and claime whatsoever to the Rectory of Spalding into the hands of William Sneath gent. and the rest of the ffeoffees for that purpose. To make that Resignation good (as Counsell should advise) in case the severall punctilios of law were not exactly answered in that which he then signed, as I had some cause to suspect hereupon, according to the agreement I desisted prosecuting the Articles against him at Lincolne, and truely not without some willingness; for I was so tyed up to a personall appearance every Courtday and his interest there was soe great that the employment was likely to growe very troublesome. I therefore rather chose to sit downe with a bare conquest then to run the hazard of a long contest and uncertaine victory, for he spared not to tell me that I could never doe him the least prejudice at Lincolne. When or whom the ffeoffees will present to your Lordship I cannot divine, but very earnest Mr Peirson is with me to intersede for him to your Lordship for the granting him a Lycence to preach, but that I must wholly to leave to your Lordships pleasure after the receiveing such satisfaction from him for his former misdeamenours as your Lordship sees fiting to require, but for his preaching any more at Spalding (unless it be a Recantation Sermon) I confesse the reason why doth not as yet apeare to me, for certainly it cannot but doe hurt where his faction is so considerable that within these four dayes he told me if he might but continue in the house and have leave to preach we should dispose of the tythes how we pleased, for he could live better without them then with them; He expresses great desire for a Lycence to keepe Schoole here, which truely I think there is noe great need of, we having severall Schooles in Towne besides our ffree Schoole and the like provision there is for most Townes about us.

It is possible if he get a lycence before the Church be filled a Major part of the ffeoffees may present him againe and then our business would begin de novo, soe that though the ruining of his fortune be not any peice of my designe, yet by his totall removall to secure the peace of the Church in this Parish may I hope be lawfully endeavoured. But I leave the whole affaire before Your Lordship, hopeing that as your honour hath been hytherto pleased to stand by us in assisting the carrying on of our business against this factious Parson and our two Church-wardens, soe your Lordship will vouchsafe to continue the same favour unto us till we manifest ourselves guilty of somewhat that may be unbecoming (which we trust in God though we never shall) the dutyes of

Your Lordships humble Servants
Anthony Oldfeild

[pp. 19–20]

APPENDIX THREE

THE LINCOLNSHIRE DEPUTY LIEUTENANTS

PRO SP 29/11/169.[1]

George Viscount Castleton[2]
Robert Lord Willoughby of Earsby
Sir Francis Fane
Sir John Monson[3]
Sir William Thorold
Sir Charles Bolles
Sir Philip Tirwhitt[4]
Sir William Hickman
Sir Thomas Hussey
Sir John Walpole
Adrian Scrope
Henry Heron
Sir Anthony Irby
Sir William Wray
Sir Martin Lister

LA Yarborough MS 8/2/5, 13 July 1662.

George Viscount Castleton
Robert Lord Willoughby of Earsby
William Lord Widdrington
Sir Francis Fane
Sir John Monson bt
Sir Thomas Hussey bt
Sir William Hickman bt
Sir Philip Tirwhitt bt
Sir William Thorold bt
Sir Robert Markham bt[5]
Sir William Trollop bt
Sir John Newton bt
Sir Anthony Oldfield bt

---

[1]   The list is calendared in a group of militia papers with ? August 1660 as the date. Wray was made a knight and baronet in July 1660 (*Complete Baronetage* iii. 64). Sir Charles Bolles died in February 1661 (Maddison, 152).
[2]   Proposed but not appointed were royalist supporters John Lord Belasyse, William Lord Widdrington, Sir Robert Bolles, Sir Charles Dallison and Francis Lord Parham, who became a supporter of the King. From a parliamentarian background were Edward Rossiter, Sir Edward Ayscough, Sir Martin Armyn, Thomas Hatcher: PRO SP 29/11/168.
[3]   Sir John Monson, second baronet, died in 1683.
[4]   Sir Philip Tyrwhitt, third baronet.
[5]   Sir Robert Markham, first baronet, died 2 February 1667. Sir Robert Markham, second baronet, was appointed a deputy in November 1669 (*CSPD 1668–9*, 587).

Sir Henry Heron
Sir Adrian Scrope
Sir Martin Lister
Sir John Walpole
Sir Edward Rossiter
Sir Thomas Meres
Sir Edward Dymock[6]
Lewis Palmer Esquire
Charles Pelham Esquire

LA Yarborough MS 8/2/6, 9 August 1666.[7]

George Viscount Castleton
Sir Francis Fane
Sir John Monson bt
Sir William Hickman bt
Sir William Thorold bt
Sir Robert Markham bt
Sir William Trollop bt
Sir William Wray bt
Sir John Newton bt
Sir Anthony Oldfield bt
Sir Henry Heron
Sir Adrian Scrope
Sir John Monson[8]
Sir Martin Lister
Sir Thomas Meres
Sir Robert Carr
Lewis Palmer Esq.
Charles Pelham Esq.
Henry Fines Esq.
Charles Dymock Esquire
Sir Edward Rossiter[9]
Sir Henry Belasyse[10]
Sir Philip Tirwhitt[11]
Sir Edward Ayscough[12]

6 Sir Edward Dymock died in January 1664.
7 Issued when Robert Bertie succeeded his father as the second Earl of Lindsey, as lieutenant.
8 Sir John Monson, son of the second baronet.
9 Sir Edward Rossiter is not listed on the 1666 commission but served as a deputy in 1667: OB 66.
10 Sir Henry Belasyse, son of Lord Belasyse, attended as a deputy in February 1666: OB 49. He is not listed on the 1666 commission but served in 1667: OB 66.
11 Sir Philip Tyrwhitt, fourth baronet, attended in 1667: OB 67.
12 For a discussion of the appointment of the deputies, see Introduction, pp. xii–xv.

APPENDIX FOUR

LIST OF THE HOLLAND TROOPS

Sir Anthony Oldfield

Mr Robert Ferrers
Mr George Slee
Mr John Brown
William Palmer
Robert Algakirke
Thomas Gilbert
Thomas Dickison senior
William Smith
Robert ffrances
Thomas Dickison junior
John Brown
James Sneath
William ffarrow
William Powell
Thomas ffisher
Richard Rhodes
John Melton
Richard Graves
John Woods
Robert Nurse
John Nicholson
John Spalding
Richard Wells
Thomas Hawden
Thomas Trinton
John Rook
Edward Cater
Robert Rose
William Cooper
Samuel Smyth
Roger Turner
Thomas Drewery
Thomas Tresse
William Soresby
Mathew Browne
William Pister
William Trusdell

John Melton
John Dinis
Christopher Copell
George Pibbard[1]
Robert Gray
Mr Andrew Slee
John Brown
Mr William Wilson
Mr George Caborn
Mr Daniel Rhods
Mr John Jackson Mayor[2]
ffrancis Balderston
49

Sir Edward Barkham[3]

Mr George Wright
John Letsham junior
John Copall
John Rushland
Mr John Ampleford
Mr John Bonner
Henry Mowbrey
George Hoglarner
Mr Robert Atkin
Roger Baddy
George Kippas
Edward Young
Joseph Cook
John Moor
Thomas Roath
Samuel Ward
Mathew North
John Letsham senior
John Webb
Thomas Jenkinson
Benjamin Ludlam
Thomas Cooper

[1] Unreadable letter between the P and i.
[2] Jackson was Mayor of Boston in 1666: Pishey Thompson, *The History and Antiquities of Boston* (Boston, 1856), 455.
[3] OB 5: Barkham was offered a Holland troop in July 1663.

John Mowberry
Thomas Hatcher
Stephen Moor
Peter Dixson
Thomas Mansffeild
Robert Stamock[4]
Samuel Hutchinson
Daniel Jenings
Peter Hannah
John Adams
Richard Bridges
William Watson
Stephen Bridge
Anthony Bower
James Edwards
Robert Mathers
John Thumble
Henry Arrindale
Anthony Butler
John Scath
Samuel Calverly
George Marston
John Hawkred
Benjamin Levington
John Shoply
William Mallry[5]
John Kirk
John Tompson
Thomas Etherington
Thomas Okerstone
George Smyth
John Baker
Edward Chapman
Ez: Yates
John Boswell Esquire
Francis Johnson
59

Sir Philip Harcourt[6]

Mr John Ellis
Mr Thomas Welby

Sir Anthony Irby
John Law
Mr Joseph Jackson
Mr Alexander Law
Christopher Watson
William Lyon
George Harwood
Michael Hoyes
David Iesserson
Samuel Collin
Thomas Laughton
Leo Bawtree
William Edwards
ffrancis Time
Thomas Rutland
Anthony Lunderson
Richard Whelpdale
Edward Leary
John Whytering
John Jerrie
Thomas Bate
John Harwood
John Hill
Robert Proctor
John Rookesby
Joseph Cozen
John Manby
Gervase Greenfield
James Cooke
Samuel Rookesby
Edward Nicholson
Thomas Nichols
William Bennington
Thomas Massam
William Barker
Thomas Laughton
Henry Mastin
Robert Cave
Thomas Haughton
Richard Holbilih
Henry Right
ffrancis Brewer
John Turner

---

4   Unreadable letter between m and o.
5   Obscured letter between l and r.
6   Harcourt of Stanton Harcourt (Oxon.) was elected as member for Boston in 1666. Sir Anthony Irby, member for Boston in the Convention and Cavalier Parliaments, had married Harcourt's aunt: *House of Commons 1660–90* ii. 489, 634–5.

William Brown
Henry Lee
William West
Cornet Blake
Thomas Person
Jervase Jackson
Henry Tomblinson
John Harwood
John Maultby
John Champney
Thomas ffoster
Thomas Parish
Thomas Ward
William Northen
John Wharfe
Samuel Marshall
Thomas Pinchbeck
Ernest Webb
Roger Renny
Nathaniel Jenkinson
Thomas Lodwick
William Stennet
Samuel Preston

Samuel Brown
Andrew Burton
John Tompson
Robert Malory
John Inkerson
Johnathon Seagrave
John Massome
John Tooly
William Hobson
Thomas Maine
Peter Bird
William Garrat
Thomas Bates
William Smyth
Samuel Beetson
Mr Joseph Jackson
Mr Benjamin Whyting
Mr Thomas Tooley
John Boult
Mr Joseph Whyting
89

[pp. 239–40]

INDEX OF PERSONS AND PLACES

Roman numerals refer to the pages of the introduction. Arabic numerals to the number of the letter. app. refers to the appendices.

Browne, Thomas, of Moulton, 25
Broxholme, (Capt.), 63.
Brudenell, Thomas, Earl of Cardigan, 17
Bruntall, 46
Brynes, Mr, 46
Buck, Sir John, xxii, 37, 38, 41
Buckingham, Duke of, *see* Villiers, George
Bumford, John, 85
Burgate, John, 25
Burgh le Marsh, Borough, Lincs., xxx, 63, 67
Burrell, Henry, 24, 25
Burton, Andrew, app. 4
Burton, Lincs., 54
Burton, Mr, 19
Busse, Henry, 81
Butler, Anthony, 4
Butler, 46

Caborn, Mr George, app. 4
Caistor, Caster, Lincs., 42, 46, 63
Campden, Viscount, *see* Noel
Canterbury, Archbishops of, *see* Juxon, Sheldon
Carbery, Lord, *see* Vaughan, Richard
Cardigan, Earl of, *see* Brudenell, Thomas
Cardinal, (Capt.), 63
Carr, Sir Robert, xv, xxvi, 44, 46, 49, app. 3
Carr, Sir William, ix
Carteret, Sir George, 12, 35, 75
Castleton, Viscount, *see* Saunderson
Catell, John, 81
Cater, Edward, app. 4
Cawthorpe, Robert, 11
Cecil, Elizabeth, dowager Countess of Exeter, 17
Cecil, John, Earl of Exeter, 17
Champney, John, app. 4
Chapman, Edward, app. 4
Chapel St Leonards, Chapple, Lincs., 63
Charles II, king, xxi, xxvi, 11, 19, 22, 36, 44, 48, 51, 52, 53, 60, 70, 71, 72, 76
Christian, Edward, ix, 3, 5, 10, 17, 19, 20, 44
Clarke, Richard, 11, 12
Clarke, Thomas, 25
Clarke, Mr William, 46
Clifford, Sir Thomas, 61, 64
Collin, Samuel, app. 4
Compton, Sir William, 12, 75
Coningsby, Cunsby, Lincs., 11
Cook, Joseph, app. 4
Cooke, James, app. 4
Cooke, Thomas, 25
Cooper, Anthony Ashley, Lord Ashley, 12, 40, 61, 74, 75, 77
Cooper, Thomas, app. 4
Copall, John, app. 4
Copell, Christopher, app. 4
Corby, Corby Glen, Lincs., 43
Coventry, Sir William, 61
Cozen, Joseph, app. 4
Craven, William, Lord, 64

Craycrafte, Mr John, 46
Crowland, Lincs., 82
Cunsby, *see* Coningsby

Dacres, Thomas, Lord, 17
Dale, John, 84
Dalton, Maurice, 46
Dawson, James, 25
Dawson, Thomas, 46
Deeping, Market, Lincs., xx, 40, 44
Dickinson, Thomas, senior, app. 4
Dickinson, Thomas, junior, app. 4
Dinis, John, app. 4
Dorchester, Marquis of, *see* Pierrepont
Drake, Mr, 46
Drewry, Thomas, app. 4
Dymock, Charles, xv, 63, 67, 72, app. 3
Dymock, Sir Edward, xiv n.49, xxii, xxvi, 38, app. 3

East, Nicholas, 85
Edgehill, Warwicks., xii
Edwards, James, app. 4
Edwards, William, app. 4
Egerton, John, Earl of Bridgwater, 61, 64
Ellis, Mr John, app. 4
Emerson, Alex, app. 4
Etherington, Thomas, app. 4
Exeter, Countess of ; Earl of, *see* Cecil

Fane, Sir Francis, xiv, 5, 9, 28, 29, 30, app. 3
Fane, Mildmay, Earl of Westmorland, xiv
Farrar, William, app. 4
Farrar, Mr, 42
Fens, xxvi–xxvii
Ferrers, Robert, app. 4
Fisher, Thomas, app. 4
Fishtoft, Lincs., 11
Fitzhardinge, Viscount, *see* Berkeley
Fleet, Lincs., xi
Fordbank, Lincs., 11
Fox, Sir Stephen, xxii
Frances, Robert, app. 4

Garner, James, 46
Garnor, Mr, 46
Garratt, William, app. 4
Gedney, Lincs., xxvii, 46, 47
Geddington, Northants., 48
Gilbert, Thomas, app. 4
Glen, Joseph, 25
Glen, Matthew, 25
Goodales, 46
Gooses, 46
Gophill, Lincs., 42
Gorrell, Thomas, 85
Grant, Johnathon, 46
Grantham, Lincs., xxiv, xxv, 26, 46, 62
Graves, Richard, app. 4
Greeneld, Robert, 25

INDEX OF SUBJECTS